PENGUIN BOOKS

LOVE POEMS FROM GOD

DANIEL LADINSKY was born in 1948 and raised in St. Louis, Missouri. For six years he made his home in western India, where he worked in a rural clinic free to the poor and lived with the family of Meher Baba, who some consider to have been the Christ come again. He has published three volumes of Hafiz's poetry: *The Gift*, *The Subject Tonight Is Love*, and *I Heard God Laughing*. He plans to retire to his mountain farm with his sweetheart Kathy and their four dogs and two cats.

ALSO BY DANIEL LADINSKY

The Gift
Poems by Hafiz, the Great Sufi Master

The Subject Tonight Is Love
60 Wild and Sweet Poems of Hafiz

I Heard God Laughing
Poems of Hope and Joy

A Year with Hafiz
Daily Contemplations

The Purity of Desire
100 Poems of Rumi
(with Nancy Owen Barton)

Darling I Love You
Poems from the Hearts of Our Glorious Mutts and
All Our Animal Friends
(illustrated by Patrick McDonnell)

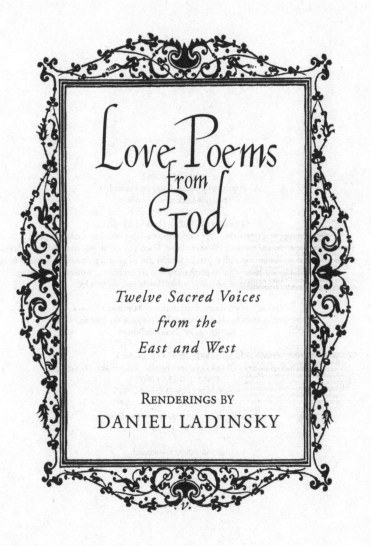

Love Poems from God

Twelve Sacred Voices
from the
East and West

RENDERINGS BY

DANIEL LADINSKY

v.

PENGUIN BOOKS

PENGUIN BOOKS
An imprint of Penguin Random House LLC
penguinrandomhouse.com

Copyright © 2002 by Daniel Ladinsky
Penguin supports copyright. Copyright fuels creativity, encourages diverse voices,
promotes free speech, and creates a vibrant culture. Thank you for buying an authorized edition
of this book and for complying with copyright laws by not reproducing, scanning, or distributing
any part of it in any form without permission. You are supporting writers and allowing
Penguin to continue to publish books for every reader.

LIBRARY OF CONGRESS CATALOGING-IN-PUBLICATION DATA
Love poems from God : twelve sacred voices from the East and West /
renderings by Daniel Ladinsky.
p.   cm.
ISBN 9780142196120 (paperback)
1. Religious poetry—Translations into English. I. Ladinsky, Daniel James.
PN6110.R4 L59 2002
808.81'9382—dc21 2002027069

PRINTED IN THE UNITED STATES OF AMERICA
1   3   5   7   9   10   8   6   4   2

Set in Adobe Garamond
Designed by M. Paul

God said,
"I am made whole by your life. Each soul,
each soul completes
me."

—Hafiz

Acknowledgments

This book would not have happened without my agent, Tom Grady. After over two years of working on it, I somewhat collapsed with a furlong to go, and he literally got it home when I was ready to give up. His name should also be on the cover, but he wouldn't let me put it there.

And Kathy, my sweetheart of seven years, do you mind if I call you Sweet Potato in public? Your astounding patience and love helped me to remove my alloy from this gold.

I thank my old buddy Alfio Grasso for his remarkable compass, and his wonderful heart and multilinguistic skills with Italian, Spanish, and Latin.

The beautiful Rumi translations by Farideh Azodi Davidson (that I one day found in my mailbox unexpectedly, while working on my chapter on Rumi) proved a grand and timely springboard for some poems in this book. I hope some publisher seeks you out, Farideh. Hint: she lives in Spruce Pine, North Carolina.

My editors at Penguin, Janet Goldstein and Jennifer Ehmann, deserve lavish thanks and kisses for their clarity and support.

And thanks to Ali Akbar Shapurzaman, Nisha Luck, Sam Kerawala, M. J., Khorshed, and General McDonald for some translations in these languages: Farsi, Hindi, Marathi, and Gujarati.

Thanks also to Father O'Farrel for giving some of these poems distemper shots.

The three hundred poems in this book were selected from over a thousand I stole from God when He made the mistake of letting me go through His files, so it seemed. Thanks, God, for not suing me. Maybe we will publish more of this wonderful contraband.

Contents

Preface

What are "love poems from God," and how can they exist? I feel that if we believe that a divine union with God is possible, then how could they not be true? "The Father and I are One," said Jesus in the Gospels. That concept, that sublime, divine experience of union with God I believe has existed since humans could conceive of time, and words similar to what Jesus spoke must have been uttered in rapturous joy in the hearts of countless souls. It has been said that just as every river is winding its way to the sea so every soul is returning to a glorious reunion with our source, God. Faith in the Ocean may be difficult at times and union may seem a fantasy, but I think the real fantasy is separateness from That which is Everywhere. "The fish in the water that is thirsty needs serious professional counseling," says one of my renderings of Kabir in this book. The water being God, the Omnipresent, and we the fish living within Him. To dismiss the possibility that the divine can speak through women and men is to limit God. As soon as we limit God's ability to communicate with us, are we not then just reinforcing some unhealthy religious prejudice, superstition, neurosis, and fear that fragments society and the individual, and undermines and divides us rather than empowers and unites? I think that all our perceptions of time and space and God are adolescent, so childish that we even go to war over them, or are at war within ourselves about some ideology; peace seems so rare these days.

Millions of people in this world believe that Rumi, St. Francis, Hafiz, Kabir, and Tukaram became divinely wed to the Infinite, achieved union with God, and thus became aspects of His voice. Others featured in this volume (their original prose now rendered into poetry) I feel were saints so void of self-interest and so full of love for God and humanity that they became holy lutes—God's "instruments," as St. Francis once said. Through their poetry, their lives, and their prayers, God played for us His music, which can still be heard today, hundreds of years later, for what a party the soul aflame creates.

Hafiz sings, "A poet is someone who can pour light into a cup, then raise it to nourish your beautiful parched holy mouth." I chose these twelve great figures to work with because of their ability to help us know our own sacredness, and because of their skill to awaken us to the wonder—and thus gratitude—of the common. "The heart suffers when it cannot see and touch beauty, but beauty is not shy, it is synonymous with existence."

I hope a few of these poems will reach in deep enough to cure what separates us from each other, and from the beautiful. I hope you fall into this wine barrel (this book) and crawl out legally drunk, and get arrested for doing something that makes God proud of you, like being too happy.

Be kind to yourself, love to all,
Daniel Ladinsky

The Genesis of These Poems

"No one could ever paint a too wonderful picture of my heart or God," says Hafiz. To nourish and free are the duty and the wonder of spiritual literature. Any liberties I have taken with these poems was an act, I hope, void of self-interest and done with the sole intention of trying to help emancipate our wings. Several translators have been helpful to me with this work, though most of what is in this book could be said to be an avant-garde portrait of these remarkable historic figures. I have used and mixed whichever of their *colors* I felt were the most genuine, the most relative to the present, and were the most capable of bringing the reader into the extraordinary experience of these great souls. For their experience of God foretells our own.

What to say to academia about these poems? Well, I think scholars have made important contributions to unveiling God, yet millions of people continue to be persecuted by frightening untruths stemming from archaic concepts of Him that took root in many of us as children. I hope there is enough benevolence—and reality—in my interpretations of these poems to alleviate some of that suffering; truth frees and makes us laugh. We need to know that God is the source of all humor and that God is Infinite Intelligence, a Beloved that does not defy our deepest sensibilities and the innate, glorious compassion of the heart.

Meher Baba once wrote, "Love and understanding never condemn but always seek to help and encourage." His words do justice to a Divine Higher Power and could be a kind of litmus test we use before we imbibe any doctrine, for what we believe surely affects us, and affects all we are connected to. And are we not connected to everything? Love does not threaten or forbid, love does not restrain our wondrous spirits or enact prohibitions. I think God loves bootleggers—defiant poets who ferment the air as they sing and lift the corners of our mouths. Words about God should never bore because God is the opposite of boring. And what we say about the Gorgeous One should make Him appear a knockout. Whoever made this universe is a Wild Guy. I think only our ecstasies offer any real clues about Him.

"No one could ever paint a too wonderful picture of . . . God." But I feel He doesn't mind that I tried. In studying the lives of these wonderful saints, I can't imagine any of them saying "no" if they were asked if we could freely adapt their words to a few bluegrass tunes or whiskey-soaked jazz. I think they might shout, "Go for it, baby; set the world on fire if you can, kick ass for the Beloved with some great art."

Love Poems from God

Rabia

When God said, "My hands are yours,"
I saw that I could heal any creature in this world;

I saw that the divine beauty in each heart
is the root of all time
and space.

Rabia of Basra (c. 717–801) is without doubt the most popular and influential of female Islamic saints and a central figure in the Sufi tradition. She was born nearly five hundred years before Rumi, and although it is rarely said, she, perhaps more than any other poet, influenced his writings.

Rabia grew up in a part of ancient Mesopotamia that is now Iraq. She was the fourth daughter of impoverished parents, and a story connected with her birth tells of the Prophet Muhammad appearing to her father in a dream to tell him that his daughter would be revered as a great saint.

The sensuousness of Rabia's poetry may be a bit shocking to some, though it was probably more so in its original. Even conservative scholarly translations cannot get around its, at times, graphic eroticism. Many myths surround her life and poems, but one has been recently confirmed by one of the most respected contemporary spiritual teachers, and may well be a source of this sensuality. When Rabia was quite young, she became separated from her parents— perhaps they died—and while wandering homeless, she was literally stolen and sold into slavery. Because of her remarkable beauty, a famous brothel bought her for a large sum, and it is believed she lived and was forced to work as one might in a brothel for many years. She wrote, "What a place for trials and transformation did my Lover put me, but never once did He look upon me as if I were impure. Dear sisters, all we do in this world, whatever happens, is bringing us closer to God."

Rabia may be a timely spiritual voice for women of this century, especially for any woman (or man) who has had to suffer the emotionally crippling degradation of unwanted touch. She was both physically and sexually abused from an early age, yet still became one of the greatest women saints—and poets—known to history.

When she was about fifty she was given her freedom, most likely bought for her by a rich patron. The remaining years of her life were devoted to meditation and prayer, and she would often see visitors seeking guidance about their lives. Many miracles are attributed to her, and apparently she was offered large sums for curing people; I like a comment attributed to her when refusing a bag of gold: "Dear, if you leave that, flies will gather as if a horse just relieved himself, and I might slip in it while dancing."

As this great woman once wrote:

Show me where it hurts, God said, and every cell in my body burst into tears before His tender eyes. He has repaid me though for all my suffering in a way I never wanted: The sun is now in homage to my face, because it knows I have seen God. But that was not His payment. The soul cannot describe His gift. I just spoke about the sun like that because I like beautiful words, and because it is true: Creation is in homage to us.

ONE DAY

One day He did not leave after
kissing
me.

OUR BEAUTY

Live with dignity, women, live with dignity, men.
Few things will more enhance our
beauty as
much.

THE PERFECT STILLNESS

Love is
the perfect stillness
and the greatest excitement, and most profound act,
and the word almost as complete
as His name.

THE WAY IT GOES

Why think God has not touched everything
that comes to your
desk?

True, He may have kept the best
for Himself.

That is just the
way it
goes.

DIE BEFORE YOU DIE

Ironic, but one of the most intimate acts
of our body is
death.

So beautiful appeared my death—knowing who then I would kiss,
I died a thousand times before I died.

"Die before you die," said the Prophet
Muhammad.

Have wings that feared ever
touched the Sun?

I was born when all I once
feared—I could
love.

THE MOMENT'S DEPTH

The moment's depth is greater than that of
the future.

And from the fields of the past, what can you harvest again?

Dried flowers I have from a meadow I laid in with her
and moved across her breasts.

When I need love's scent I touch them.

A mine with jewels can be the past
for the heart,

but who goes to an old mine that only made
you sad?

I have seen a man walk on a high stretched rope
holding a long pole for balance: memories and dreams can do that,
be a great help.

The soul does not understand the word seasons. The
petals on the sun can only be touched now.

The beauty of dried flowers, how can they
compare to
Him?

THE SKY GAVE ME ITS HEART

The sky gave me its heart
because it knew mine was not large enough to care
for the earth the way
it did.

Why is it we think of God so much?
Why is there so much talk
about love?

When an animal is wounded
no one has to tell it, "You need to heal"; so naturally it will nurse
itself the best it can.

My eye kept telling me, "Something is missing from
all I see." So it went in search of the cure.

The cure for me was His beauty, the remedy—
for me was to
love.

SLICING POTATOES

It helps,
putting my hands on a pot, on a broom,
in a wash
pail.

I
tried painting,
but it was easier to fly slicing
potatoes.

IN MY SOUL

In
my soul
there is a temple, a shrine, a mosque, a church
where I kneel.

Prayer should bring us to an altar where no walls or names exist.

Is there not a region of love where the sovereignty is
illumined nothing,

where ecstasy gets poured into itself
and becomes
lost,

where the wing is fully alive
but has no mind or
body?

In
my soul
there is a temple, a shrine, a mosque,
a church

that dissolve, that
dissolve in
God.

IT WORKS

Would you come if someone called you
by the wrong name?

I wept, because for years He did not enter my arms;
then one night I was told a
secret:

Perhaps the name you call God is
not really His, maybe it
is just an
alias.

I thought about this, and came up with a pet name
for my Beloved I never mention
to others.

All I can say is—
it works.

THEY MIGHT HOLD HANDS

Maybe if I brought the moon a little closer
lovers would argue
less.

They might hold hands outside and point to
the heavens and say,

"I think God is up to
something

sweet!"

THE WAY THE FOREST SHELTERS

I know about love the way the fields know about light,
the way the forest shelters,

the way an animal's divine raw desire seeks to unite with
whatever might please its soul—without a single
strange thought
of remorse.

There is a powerful delegation in us that
lobbies every moment for
contentment.

How will you ever find peace
unless you yield to love

the way the gracious earth
does to our hand's
impulse.

MY POEMS ATTEMPT

All
of what
I would want my child to know
my poems attempt.

We are infants before each other, are we not,
so vulnerable to each other's words and
movements.

A school I sat in cured me of hurting others.

I have come to see that all are seated at His table, and I
have become His
servant.

Sometimes God is too shy to speak in public
and He pinches me.

That
is my cue—
to fill in the blanks of your
understanding

the best I
can.

IF I DID NOT PRAY

I could not move against this wind if I did not pray.
And all that is said of me that is untrue
would make lame my gait if I
could not free myself from
the weight of other's
malice.

I could not move against all His light
if I did not
pray.

See how things become: what a change
can happen, when we find a way
to keep Him
close.

TRYING TO WORK IN

Once I heard two camels talking,
they were complaining about all the weight they had to carry
when they crossed the desert,

and they were especially peeved about that new camel whose only
load was the master's young daughter who would often
pet the camel and even sing to it sweet songs,

while they had to often feel the whip of men
and listen to them tell crude stories of romantic exploits.

An older camel was overhearing the chat, as I was, and spoke
saying,
"You know, it is our habit to bite when we are grouchy and
just yesterday I saw you snap at that man who whipped you—
maybe you shouldn't bite; maybe the master has two
daughters who sing and pet,
and although this may be stretching things a bit
I am reminded of some words of wisdom
I have been trying to work in
somewhere,
for days:

Those who are trusted by others
God trusts."

CHERISH MYSELF

I know how it will be when I die,
my beauty will be so extraordinary that God will worship me.
He will not worship me from a distance, for our minds will have wed,
our souls will have flowed into each other.
How to say this: God and I
will forever cherish
Myself.

JEALOUS OF A POND

When God said, "My hands are yours," I saw that I could heal any
creature in this world;

I saw that the divine beauty in each heart
is the root of all time
and space.

I was once a sleeping ocean
and in a dream became
jealous of a
pond.

A penny can be eyed in the street
and a war can break out
over it amongst
the poor.

Until we know that God lives in us
and we can see Him
there,

a great poverty
we suffer.

I HOPE GOD THINKS LIKE THAT

There is a dog I sometimes take for a walk
and turn loose in a
field,

when I can't give her that freedom
I feel in debt.

I hope God thinks like that and

is keeping track of all
the bliss He
owes
me.

IT ACTS LIKE LOVE

It acts like love—music,
it reaches toward the face, touches it, and tries to let you know
His promise: that all will be okay.

It acts like love—music, and
tells the feet, "You do not have to be so burdened."

My body is covered with wounds
this world made,

but I still longed to kiss Him, even when God said,

"Could you also kiss the hand that caused
each scar,

for you will not find me until
you do."

It does that—music—helps us
to forgive.

THE MOON WAS ONCE A MOTH

The moon was once a moth who ran to her lover,
they embraced, and she ultimately passed away
with such a smile everywhere on
her body.

Over a period of time, her wings fell to the earth
and sanctified the meadows.
Angels came and buried the limbs
that touched His mouth.

The moon was once a moth who ran to God,
they entwined.

Now just her luminous soul remains
and we gaze at it
at night.

A VASE

I am always holding a priceless vase in my hands.
If you asked me about the deeper truths
of the path and I told you
the answers,

it would be like handing sacred relics to you.
But most have their hands tied
behind their
back;

that is, most are not free of events their eyes have seen

and their ears have heard

and their bodies have felt.

Most cannot focus their abilities
in the present, and
might drop what
I said.

So I'll wait; I don't mind waiting until
your love for all
makes luminous
the now.

A BREAST IN THE SKY

I hear talk about the famous.
I hear talk about different cities.

The most intimate events of families come to my ears.
I hear about temples and
mosques and
saints.

All that can be said I have heard.
All that can be wanted I
have seen.

My interest in this world has waned, though
not because I am
depressed.

A fish in a bowl I was,
a bottom feeder,

but now I nurse
upon a breast
in the
sky.

COULD YOU WAIT TILL FOUR?

My understanding used to be like a stream
that easily described all along the bank as its ken moved
through the world.

When I entered God, my vision became like His,
it flooded out over existence,
I knew no limits.

The future I can now see with as much certainty
as the past.

If I stretched my arm its full length
I could caress any creature in this universe;
and Rabia does not
exaggerate.

Thus going to bed one night
I knew a thief would be breaking
in at 3 A.M.,

so I wrote a note and put it on my door,
that said,

"Could you wait till 4?"

for the passion in prayers
usually starts to wane
by then.

A LOVER WHO WANTS HIS LOVERS NEAR

He is
sweet that way,
trying to coax the world to dance.

Look how the wind holds the trees in its hands
helping them to
sway.

Look how the sky takes the fields and the oceans
and our bodies in its arms, and moves
all beings toward
His lips.

God must get hungry for us; why is He not also
a lover who wants His lovers
near?

Beauty
is my teacher
helping me to know He
cares for
me.

TROUBLEMAKERS

Since no one really knows anything about God,

those who think they do are just

troublemakers.

THIS CHOIR

So amazing this choir of
socks, shoes, shirt, skirt, undergarments,

earth, sky, suns, and
moons.

No wonder I too, now,
sing all
day.

St. Francis of Assisi

No one lives outside the walls of this sacred place, existence.

Francis Bernardone (1182–1226) is the most beloved saint of the Western world. His love for nature and his hymns to the sun, moon, earth, and birds have captured the hearts of millions of Catholics, and the respect of millions of people of all faiths. This saint achieved the highest state of consciousness possible to man, a divine union with God.

Francis was born in 1182, in Assisi in central Italy, into the family of a wealthy linen merchant, Pietro di Bernardone. In his youth he enjoyed all the privileges of such a station in life, and was said to have especially loved parties. The end of the twelfth century was a time of political turmoil, and as Francis grew to manhood he began to embrace the ideals of medieval chivalry as depicted in the troubadours' songs, influencing him to seek a military career as a knight. He was captured and imprisoned after his first battle (between Assisi and Perugia), and returned home a year later, very ill. Recovered, he determined to enlist again, this time fighting for the pope in the Crusades. The Crusades brought Francis to the Middle East, and there are accounts that St. Francis was in contact with Rumi's master, Shams, while Francis was in Damascus. Francis had many visions in his life, and it was around this time that one of these visions made him realize a military career was not for him. He returned home and began a new life, on fire with love for God. He began to devote himself to helping the impoverished and the afflicted. It is said that he embraced and kissed a leper, and experienced a baptism of joy and triumph over fear.

There are many wonderful accounts of St. Francis. When he was about twenty-five, he would often pray in secluded spots. Once while in an old country chapel, the painted figure of Christ on the crucifix spoke to him, saying, "Francis, go and repair my house, which, as you see, is falling completely to ruin." Thus, his destiny began to unfold.

Another story that may be unfamiliar to some readers is that sometimes when Francis was traveling with his brother monks he would pick up a stick and pretend it was a violin bow and his arm a violin, and he would start playing *the violin* and singing French songs that his mother had taught him as a child. Francis would leap about and dance and become ecstatic. It is said of Francis that his love for God at times made him so wild that few understood him.

In many churches around the world one of the happiest Sundays is St. Francis Day, when people bring their animals to the church to be blessed. St. Francis's life was a great blessing to all. His spiritual beauty, power, and compassion will always offer us guidance.

BECAUSE HE GAVE BIRTH

So
precious
is a person's faith in God,
so precious;

never should we harm
that.

Because
He gave birth
to all

religions.

WHEN I RETURNED FROM ROME

A
bird took flight.
And a flower in a field whistled at me
as I passed.

I drank
from a stream of clear water.
And at night the sky untied her hair and I fell asleep
clutching a tress
of God's.

When I returned from Rome, all said,
"Tell us the great news,"

and with great excitement I did: "A flower in a field whistled,
and at night the sky untied her hair and
I fell asleep clutching a
sacred tress . . ."

HE ASKED FOR CHARITY

God came to my house and asked for charity.
And I fell on my knees and
cried, "Beloved,

what may I
give?"

"Just love," He said.
"Just love."

A KIND FACE

Joy is the greatest cleanser, and it is
the greatest testimony to our
faith.

"Toil with happiness," my Lord once
said to me.

God sent a servant on an errand
through a dangerous part
of the world.

The servant, having received in hand
what God wanted
delivered,

turned to the Holy and said,
"My Beloved Master, do you have a final instruction?"
and God replied,

"A kind face is a
precious
gift."

THE HOLY WATER

No one lives outside the walls of this sacred place, existence.
The holy water, I need it upon my eyes: it is you, dear, you—each form.

What mother would lose her infant—and we are that to God,
never lost from His gaze are we? Every cry of the heart
is attended by light's own arms.

You cannot wander anywhere that will not aid you.
Anything you can touch—God brought it into
the classroom of your mind.

Differences exist, but not in the city of love.
Thus my vows and yours, I know they are the same.

I have just peeled the skin from the potato
and you are still contemplating its worth,
sweetheart; indeed there are wonderful nutrients in all,
for God made everything.

You joined our community at birth.
With your Father being who He is, what do the
world's scales know of your precious value.
The priest and the prostitute—they weigh the same before the Son's
immaculate being,
but who can bear that truth and freedom,
so a wise man adulterated the
scriptures;
every wise man knows this.

My soul's face has revealed its beauty to me;
why was it shy so long, didn't it know how this made me suffer
and weep?

A different game He plays with His close ones.
God tells us truths you would not believe,
for most everyone needs to limit His compassion; concepts of
right and wrong preserve the golden seed
until one of God's friends comes along and tends your body
like a divine bride.

The Holy sent out a surveyor to find the limits of its compassion
and being.
God knows a divine frustration whenever He acts like that,
for the Infinite has
no walls.

Why not tease Him about this?
Why not accept the freedom of what it means
for our Lord to see us
as Himself.

So magnificently sovereign is our Lover; never say,
"On the other side of this river a different king rules."
For how could that be true—for nothing can oppose Infinite strength.

No one lives outside the walls of this sacred place, existence.

The holy water my soul's brow needs is unity.
Love opened my eye and I was cleansed
by the purity of each
form.

HUMILITY AND COMPASSION

Can true humility and compassion exist in our words and eyes
unless we know we too are capable of
any act?

ALWAYS FROM THE CHILD'S HAND

Always from the child's hand the sword
should be removed.

I think every nation is
an infant.

NO ONE KNOWS HIS NAME

No one
knows his name—
a man who lives on the streets
and walks around in
rags.

Once I saw that man in a dream.
He and God were constructing
an extraordinary
temple.

LIKE ROOTS

Our hands imbibe like roots,
so I place them on what is beautiful in this world.

And I fold them in prayer, and they
draw from the heavens
light.

GOD WOULD KNEEL DOWN

I think God might be a little prejudiced.
For once He asked me to join Him on a walk
through this world,

and we gazed into every heart on this earth,
and I noticed He lingered a bit longer
before any face that was
weeping,

and before any eyes that were
laughing.

And sometimes when we passed
a soul in worship

God too would kneel
down.

I have come to learn: God
adores His
creation.

ANYONE WHO SUFFERED

I
would not
leave this earth until God
promised
me
that my hands could always touch the face of
anyone who
suffered.

IN HIS SANITY

If all the tenderness in this world could reflect
from my eyes, would you accept
that love?

If all
the forgiveness
the heavens have known could be offered
from one
face,

would you accept that
divine pardon?

In His sublime sanity—
every moment God offers
that to
us:

anything that might
comfort.

A WEDDING GIFT

I hear you singing, dear, inviting me to your limb.
I am coming, for all that we do is a
preparation for
love.

I hear you singing, my Lord, inviting me to your throne.
We are coming, dear, for all the toil you have
blessed us with
is a preparation to know and hold the
sacred.

I hear you singing, my soul, but how can it be that
God's voice has now become
my own?

"That is just a wedding gift for our
Divine Union,"

my Beloved
said.

OUR NEED FOR THEE

In our ever present need for thee: Beloved, let us know your peace.
Let us be your instruments that break every shackle,
for do not the caged ones weep.

And give us our inheritance of divine love so that we can forgive
like you. And let us be wise, so that we do not wed another's
madness and then make them in debt to us for the deep gash their
helpless raging lance will cause.

Darkness is an unlit wick; it just needs your touch, Beloved, to
become a sacred flame. And what sadness in this world could
endure if it looked into your eyes?

God is like a honeybee, He doesn't mind me calling Him that; for
when you are kind—sweet—He nears, and can draw you into
Himself.

What is there to understand of each other: if a wand turned the
sun into a moon would not the moon mourn the ecstatic
effulgence it once was. We are all in mourning for the experience
of our essence we knew and now miss. Light is the cure, all
else a placebo.

Yes, I will console any creature before me that is not laughing or
full of passion for their art or life; for laughing and passion—
beauty and joy—is our heart's truth, all else is labor and foreign to
the soul.

I have stood in His rain and now fill granaries as do the fertile
plains; giving is as natural to love as sound from the mouth.

There is a courageous dying, it is called effacement. That holy
death unfurls our spirit's wings and allows us to embrace God even
as we stand on the earth.

DOES EVERY CREATURE HAVE A SOUL?

A tool
in your hand I am, dear God,
the sweetest instrument you have shaped my being into.

What makes me now complete—
feeling the soul of every creature against
my heart.

Does every creature have a
soul?

Surely they do; for anything God has touched
will have life
forever,

and all creatures He
has held.

WILD FORCES

There are beautiful wild forces within us.

Let them turn the mills inside
and fill
sacks

that feed even
heaven.

WRING OUT MY CLOTHES

Such love does
the sky now pour,
that whenever I stand in a field,

I have to wring out the light
when I get
home.

GOD'S ADMIRATION

God's admiration for us is infinitely greater
than anything we can conjure up
for Him.

ONLY LOVE HONORS GOD

Only love honors God.
That sounds as if it could be true.

But surely everything He
made must be
perfect.

OF COURSE I AM JEALOUS

We bless the earth with each step we take.
And the firmament too needs
our touch:

someday your tenderness
will reach it.

Look how the birds climb some invisible staircase
and lay their hands upon Him.
Of course I am jealous,
when I too cannot
do that.

The seas waited long to sing. Not until we leaped out laughing
was their birth of us
complete.

"Tell me about your heart," my every word says.
Speak to me as if we both lay wounded
in a field and are gazing
in wonder

as our spirits
rise.

IN ALL THINGS

It was easy to love God in all that
was beautiful.

The lessons of deeper knowledge, though, instructed me
to embrace God in all
things.

THE SACRAMENTS

I once spoke to my friend, an old squirrel, about the Sacraments—
he got so excited

and ran into a hollow in his tree and came
back holding some acorns, an owl feather,
and a ribbon he had found.

And I just smiled and said, "Yes, dear,
you understand:

everything imparts
His grace."

THE RESULT OF PRAYER

The result of prayer is life.

Prayer irrigates the
earth and
heart.

IN A VISION

I asked for the most intimate experience with the Christ.

No one would believe what happened
in a vision more true than
this world:

The
sacred chord
pulsated light throughout the universe
as I nursed my own
Lord at my
breasts.

DEAR GOD

Dear God, please reveal to us
your sublime
beauty

that is everywhere, everywhere, everywhere,

so that we will never again
feel frightened.

My divine love, my love,
please let us touch
your face.

Rumi

*On a day when the wind is perfect the sail just needs to open
and the world is full of beauty. Today is such a day.*

Jalaludin Rumi (1207–1273) is considered one of the greatest
poets known to history. His influence throughout the Islamic world
for over seven hundred years and more recently in Western coun-
tries is astounding. He is currently one of the most widely read po-
ets in the English language.

Rumi was born September 30, 1207, in Balkh, Afghanistan,
which was at that time considered the eastern edge of the Persian
empire. When he was about eight years old his family was forced to
flee from the invasion of the Mongol armies of Genghis Khan. They
settled in Konya, Turkey, where Rumi remained for the rest of his
life. His father, Bahauddin Walad, a scholar and a mystic, became
the head (sheikh) of a dervish college (a divinity school). Rumi suc-
ceeded to this position upon his father's death and often would read
to his students from his father's mystical diary/testament, *Maarif.*

There are several accounts of the momentous event in Rumi's
life, his transformation, which began in 1244 when he meet Shams.
Shams, a wandering dervish from Tabriz, was on a quest for the
one spiritual companion to whom he could bequeath his spiritual
legacy. He wove a path through vagabonds and street people, always
slipping away at the slightest hint of admiration. One account of
their meeting describes Rumi reading from the *Maarif* while sitting
in a public square in Konya. Shams suddenly appeared from among
the crowd and grabbed the diary as well as several other sacred texts

and threw them into a nearby fountain. Rumi was aghast, fearing his precious books would be ruined. Shams then retrieved the books, showing Rumi they were perfectly dry and then giving Rumi the choice between scholarship through text or living sacred experience. Rumi chose the latter, suddenly realizing that he had come face to face with the doorway to God.

Thus began a relationship of divine union. Shams, sensing that their indefinable association was causing jealousy among Rumi's students, suddenly disappeared as swiftly as he had first appeared. It has been said that this was when Rumi first began expressing himself through poetry—expressing the pangs of separation from Shams as well as the ecstatic love he had been initiated into. He also began to blissfully dance—to whirl—and is known as the founder of the Whirling Dervishes.

Rumi sent his son to bring Shams back to him. They were reunited and had almost four more years together, during which time Shams lived in Rumi's home. One night in 1248, Shams disappeared, never to be seen again. (He was probably murdered by one of Rumi's jealous students.) Rumi was inconsolable and began wandering, searching for any trace of his friend who was All-in-All to him. Finally he realized that his beloved Shams was within him. He felt it was Shams who was writing the poetry, and even entitled his collected poems *The Works of Shams of Tabriz*. This collection contains some 40,000 verses; and his *Mathnawi*, which he spent the last twelve years of his life transmitting to his closest student, was another 25,000 to 30,000 verses. He died on December 17, 1273.

Some say Rumi would not have gifted such an enormous literary treasure to the world without Shams, his teacher, and a sacred longing to unite with the *Hidden* that took place when Shams disappeared. But that is exactly the role of a Master, to create an intense desire for union with the Beloved—and when union happens an atomic mystical power is released that can be directed toward humanity.

Rumi says to us in a poem, "Love is the cure, for your pain will keep giving birth to more pain until your eyes constantly exhale love as effortlessly as your body yields its scent." Love is the essence of Rumi, love became his very being, love is the impetus of all his poetry. Rumi sings fantastic promises that do not disappoint the sincere student. "Stand with dignity in the magnificent current of my words and they will carry you into God's arms."

WHERE AM I GOING?

Where am I going on this glorious journey?

To your house, of

course.

WITH PASSION

With

passion pray. With

passion work. With passion make love.

With passion eat and drink and dance and play.

Why look like a dead fish

in this ocean

of

God?

ISN'T THAT SOMETHING?

I
like when
the music happens like this:

Something in His eye grabs hold of a
tambourine in
me,

then I turn and lift a violin in someone else,
and they turn, and this turning
continues;

it has
reached you now. Isn't that
something?

GAINFUL EMPLOYMENT

These just
aren't words you are reading.
If you churn them, you could have some
good cream.

If you kept working with my poems,
you could open up a shop
and sell the finest
butter.

If you fell in love with Rumi
you could give gainful employment
to your family

and have fun together
hawking my
wonderful
cheese.

NIBBLE AT ME

Nibble at me.

Don't gulp me down.

How often is it you have a guest in your house

who can fix everything?

THAT LIVES IN US

If you put your hands on this oar with me,
they will never harm another, and they will come to find
they hold everything you want.

If you put your hands on this oar with me, they would no longer
lift anything to your
mouth that might wound your precious land—
that sacred earth that is
your body.

If you put your soul against this oar with me,
the power that made the universe will enter your sinew
from a source not outside your limbs, but from a holy realm
that lives in us.

Exuberant is existence, time a husk.
When the moment cracks open, ecstasy leaps out and devours space;
love goes mad with the blessings, like my words give.

Why lay yourself on the torturer's rack of the past and future?
The mind that tries to shape tomorrow beyond its capacities
will find no rest.

Be kind to yourself, dear—to our innocent follies.
Forget any sounds or touch you knew that did not help you dance.
You will come to see that all evolves us.

If you put your heart against the earth with me, in serving
every creature, our Beloved will enter you from our sacred realm
and we will be, we will be
so happy.

THE WAY WINGS SHOULD

What will
our children do in the morning?
Will they wake with their hearts wanting to play,
the way wings
should?

Will they have dreamed the needed flights and gathered
the strength from the planets that all men and women need to balance
the wonderful charms of
the earth

so that her power and beauty does not make us forget our own?

I know all about the ways of the heart—how it wants to be alive.

Love so needs to love
that it will endure almost anything, even abuse,
just to flicker for a moment. But the sky's mouth is kind,
its song will never hurt you, for I
sing those words.

What will our children do in the morning
if they do not see us
fly?

RUMI, PAY HOMAGE

If God said,

"Rumi, pay homage to everything
that has helped you
enter my
arms,"

there would not be one experience of my life,
not one thought, not one feeling,
not any act, I
would not
bow
to.

RELATIONSHIP BOOSTER

Here is a relationship booster
that is guaranteed to
work:

Every time your spouse or lover says something stupid
make your eyes light up as if you

just heard something

brilliant.

THE CHANCE OF HUMMING

A
man
standing on two logs in a river
might do all right floating with the current
while humming in the
now.

Though
if one log is tied to a camel,
who is also heading south along the bank—at the same pace—
all could still be well
with the
world

unless the camel
thinks he forgot something, and
abruptly turns upstream,
then

uh-oh.

Most minds
do not live in the present
and can stick to a reasonable plan; most minds abruptly turn
and undermine the

chance

of

humming.

§ 71 §

SPIRITUAL HEALTH

A good gauge of spiritual health is to write down

the three things you most want.

If they in any way differ,

you are in trouble.

OKAY, I'LL DO IT

Okay, I will do it:
sing longer songs tonight because sometimes
you're just so damn hard to please, and I guess I am
still courting you, trying to get into
your soul's knickers.

What makes you like that—grouchy around the edges?
What classrooms have you lounged in;
what nonsense have you traded
your gold
for?

How can you look so needy—
God is growing in fields you own.

He hangs from trees you pass every day. He is disguised as that
peach and pine cone.

Every sound I hear—He made it.

I have been walking with two canes these days—
guess why?

It is because of His beauty and that blond peach fuzz floating
everywhere like dust—

it has made me
so drunk.

THE SILK WORM

I stood before a silk worm one day.
And that night my heart said to me,

"I can do things like that, I can spin skies,
I can be woven into love that can bring warmth to people;
I can be soft against a crying face,
I can be wings that lift, and I can travel on my thousand feet
throughout the earth,
my sacks filled
with the
sacred."

And I replied to my heart,

"Dear, can you really do all those things?"

And it just nodded "Yes"
in silence.

So we began and will never
cease.

I AM AFRAID OF THE DAYLIGHT

All these miracles are about to drive me crazy:

my elbows, my ears, my nose, my wife's nagging,
and the sweet darkness of the night, and this blanket existence
around my soul,
and my heart connected to the pulse of
every creature.

I am afraid of the daylight.
Yesterday God was
everywhere

throwing

bliss

balls, planets, and
their kin.

HOW DOES GOD KEEP FROM FAINTING?

The wonder of water moving over that rock in the stream
justifies existence.

The swish of a horse's tail—again I am stunned
by the grandeur of the unseen One
that governs all
movement.

I resist looking at the palms of my hands sometimes.
Have you ever gotten breathless before a beautiful face,
for I see you there,
my dear.

There is a wonderful problem waiting for you
that God and I share:

how to keep from fainting when we
see each other.

In truth:

how does God keep from fainting
looking at Himself all day?

Light is moving like a stream, and
the myriad celestial beings
applaud.

BELLY DANCER

Most poets are like a belly dancer
who never reveals anything below her waist—

I won't tease you like that
for I love when your
eyes get

e
x
c
i
t
e
d.

ON A DAY WHEN THE WIND IS PERFECT

On a day
when the wind is perfect,
the sail just needs to open and the world is full of beauty.
Today is such a
day.

My eyes are like the sun that makes promises:
the promise of life
that it always
keeps

each morning.

The living heart gives to us as does that luminous sphere,
both caress the earth with great
tenderness.

There is a breeze that can enter the soul.
This love I know plays a drum. Arms move around me;
who can contain their self before my beauty?

Peace is wonderful,
but ecstatic dance is more fun, and less narcissistic;
gregarious He makes our lips.

On a day when the wind is perfect,
the sail just needs to open
and the love starts.

Today is such
a day.

HUDDLED BENEATH THE SKY

The sadness I have caused any face
by letting a stray word
strike it,

any pain
I have caused you,
what can I do to make us even?
Demand a hundredfold of me—I'll pay it.

During the day I hold my feet accountable
to watch out for wondrous insects and their dwellings.

Why would I want to bring horror
into their extraordinary
world?

Magnetic fields draw us to Light; they move our limbs and thoughts.
But it is still dark; if our hearts do not hold a lantern,
we will stumble over each other,

huddled beneath the sky
as we are.

HEY

The grass beneath a tree is content
and silent.

A squirrel holds an acorn in its praying hands,
offering thanks, it looks like.

The nut tastes sweet; I bet the prayer spiced
it up somehow.

The broken shells fall on the grass,
and the grass looks up
and says,
"Hey."

And the squirrel looks down
and says,

"Hey."

I have been saying "Hey" lately too,
to God.

Formalities just weren't
working.

CAN YOU BECOME SUCH A KING?

I want that kind of grace from God
that when it hits

I won't get off the floor for days. And when I finally
do stagger into a semblance of poise

I will still need a cane and shoulder to help me walk, and I will need
great patience from any who try to decipher
my slurred speech.

You should forget about knowing the Friend unless
you are willing to kiss the world with
great abandon.

Locked like a pair of dogs,
openly making love
in the streets,

impervious to shouts and pails of water being thrown
and glares from eyes
that pass.

Can you become such an
ego-less
king?

DECEIVE OUR GLORY

Something inside said I was a mineral, and I was so glad to just be,
I replied, "I'll take that job; it sounds like fun."

But after eons, roots appeared on my soul that wanted to nurse
from a warm body, and the wonder of her love, the tenderness
of the earth lifted me into the air and I beheld
light, and praised it from
the fields.

Time sculpted my senses and another song I heard,
"You are more than plant, you are like those
extraordinary beasts,"

so I believed that and roamed and roamed, but then I
started thinking: What is my real
truth?

I became the wings on falcons and angels.
I flirted with God in the sky.

And I believed that He, once in a while kissing me,
would be as close to love as I would get,
but now I know:

All words and images deceive
our glory.

IT'S RIGGED

It's rigged—everything, in your favor.
So there is nothing to worry about.

Is there some position you want,
some office, some acclaim, some award, some con, some lover,
maybe two, maybe three, maybe four—all at once,

maybe a relationship
with
God?

I know there is a gold mine in you, when you find it
the wonderment of the earth's gifts you will lay
aside as naturally as does
a child a
doll.

But, dear, how sweet you look to me kissing the unreal;
comfort, fulfill yourself in any way possible—do that until
you ache, until you ache,

then come to me
again.

MY LIPS GOT LOST

My lips got lost on the way to the kiss—
that's how drunk I
was.

Luckily though I still connected
with the most tender part
of her.

The moon conceived—what
a wild looking baby
we are going to
have.

I GUESS YOU WON'T MIND

Great lions can find peace in a cage.
But we should only do that
as a last
resort.

So those bars I see that restrain your wings,
I guess you won't mind
if I pry them
open.

BLOOD SUCKERS FROM HELL

Rumi speaking to a crowd muses:

Watch out for those blood suckers from hell—
cause they're everywhere.

And the crowd wisely retorts:
"That sounds serious—what do they look like, any hints;
are they usually disguised?"

Rumi again: Yes, usually, they are awful tricky!

"How then to detect them?"

Well,
I have noticed
their eyes will narrow and their faces begin to squint
like prunes

if they hear good
poetry.

Meister Eckhart

A hand in my soul can reach out and touch Jerusalem
as my other hand tastes the beauty of the Rhine.

Meister Eckhart (1260–1328) is one of history's great mystics. His religious writings were so eloquent that they helped evolve the German language. He was a Catholic monk and scholar who often presented his faith and spiritual understandings in sermons of stunning clarity, though the Catholic Church apparently feared Eckhart's brilliance and was on the verge of bringing him before a kind of inquisition when he died. The works of Meister Eckhart are a theological treasure. They are perhaps, at times, even divine revelation.

Meister Eckhart was born in the village of Hochheim, in Germany. When he was a young man he joined the Dominicans at Erfurt. He superbly blended the life of contemplation within a career of great external involvement. He became a teacher, and then in 1298 was made prior of the Dominican convent at Erfurt and vicar-provincial of Thuringia. In 1300 he began to lecture in Paris and two years later was given the degree of Master of Sacred Theology by his order. When he returned to Erfurt, he was made provincial for the large province of Saxony, and later he was appointed vicar-general for Bohemia and was asked to reform the demoralized monasteries there. In 1311 he again went to Paris and took up a professorship. He was made first professor of his order at Cologne in 1320 and remained there for the rest of his life. He was considered by many the ideal priest and scholar.

It was life itself that Eckhart loved to talk about: the life of the fields and the life of the sky, and the wonders of the human heart. It is easy to see how he raised many a brow when he spoke out like this: *"Is this not a holy trinity: the firmament, the earth, our bodies. And is it not an act of worship to hold a child, and till the soil and lift a cup. And Communion, first seek that from your lover's soul before anything offered from a priest."*

His deep and radical insights and his great popularity with his countrymen led to accusations of heresy. Eckhart publicly defended himself in February of 1327, stating that he had always believed God was as God said He was—Indivisible. And that sincere contemplation of God's own description of Himself turned into the sublime experiences and compassionate understanding that he (Eckhart) preached and wrote about.

Eckhart died the following year. The Church condemned and suppressed his work, and probably destroyed a lot of it. In the 1880s two Latin manuscripts of Eckhart's were found. Since 1980 the Dominican Order has sought to reveal that Eckhart was an exemplary Christian mystic and priest.

WHEN I WAS THE FOREST

When I was the stream, when I was the
forest, when I was still the field,
when I was every hoof, foot,
fin and wing, when I
was the sky
itself,

no one ever asked me did I have a purpose, no one ever
wondered was there anything I might need,
for there was nothing
I could not
love.

It was when I left all we once were that
the agony began, the fear and questions came,
and I wept, I wept. And tears
I had never known
before.

So I returned to the river, I returned to
the mountains. I asked for their hand in marriage again,
I begged—I begged to wed every object
and creature,

and when they accepted,
God was ever present in my arms.
And He did not say,
"Where have you
been?"

For then I knew my soul—every soul—
has always held
Him.

THE WIND WILL SHOW ITS KINDNESS

A man
born blind can easily
deny the magnificence of a vast landscape.

He can easily deny all the wonders that he cannot touch,
smell, taste, or hear.

But one day the wind will show its kindness
and remove the tiny patches that
cover your eyes,

and you will see God more clearly
than you have ever seen
yourself.

A FLAME BURNED WELL

A flame
burned well and kept its country warm.

There weren't many inhabitants in that world.
A spider lived in a cozy web in the corner of the window.

She felt the warmth from the candle on the sill
and slept better at night.

And they visited sometimes, three moths, and
pressed against the
pane

I look out from onto
God.

WHY SO MANY SOULS?

When were you last really happy?
Let that experience ferment,
bring it to mind once
in a while.

Surely in the genesis of that past moment, when you danced,
you would not have wanted a constable
to have knocked
on your
door,

or have said, "You just entered
a restricted ground."

Why are there so many stars and souls,
with no end in sight for
them?

Because nothing can interrupt God
when He is having
fun,

creating!

JERUSALEM

A hand in my soul can reach out and touch Jerusalem
as my other hand tastes the beauty of the Rhine.

And my bare foot can stand upon the holy ashes of rain—each drop a
fallen Phoenix—that sang out from the fire of union
with clay.

The hills, the valleys, the beasts, the vineyards, the sacred meadows
on our earth and body—they shall pass and ascend as all form does,
tiring of the space within a cage;

for all crowds the soul but the infinite. Ascenders to God we are.

Look though how we enrich this planet with our melting organic
shadows, wondrous shadows are all but He.

What a womb God has—what wild love He must have made to
Himself for days and days without stopping

to have given birth to all you can imagine, and to all you cannot
conceive.

Draw a circle around the frontiers of space, barely can God fit a
toe there.

All language has taken an oath to fail to describe Him;
any attempt to do so is the height of arrogance and will
always declare some kind of war:
the inner ones that undermine our strength, and the outer conflicts
that maim red.

I cried out one night in the madness of separation from love,
in the madness of doing, of trying to add to the Perfect;
for Perfect is All.

The awakened heart is like a luminous sphere—just giving without
thought to any who may come close or gaze at it.
The soul becomes blessedly lost to all
but its own holy
being.

When we cannot be who we are our divine senses become mute,
mute and sick from the insanity of judging
what He made Immaculate.

Who must God have made love to in order to have given birth to
all this sound,
to this sacred spectrum of color, scents, and music from the
wind's body and existence's plea for mercy—that
plea for the real mercy, unbearable joy?

Once we had four legs and tails so useful to balance our raid into
heaven, and I found them again.

I am a swimming galaxy tonight. Angels prowl around me
hoping I will toss them a fresh piece of light—
here dears, here, my sack is full.

The universe rents space from me, and oceans are drawn
from my well. How can that be?

For I can touch Jerusalem while my other hand tastes
the beauty of the
Rhine.

Yes, I can kiss Jerusalem while my mouth
tastes the wonders of
the Rhine.

HE TOLD ME A JOKE

My Lord told me a joke.

And seeing Him laugh has done more for me
than any scripture I will
ever read.

ALWAYS KISSING

They are always kissing, they can't
control themselves.

It is not possible
that any creature can have greater instincts
and perceptions than the
mature human
mind.

God
ripened me.
So I see it is true:
all objects in existence are
wildly in
love.

INTIMATE

Knowledge always deceives.

It always limits the Truth, every concept and image does.

From cage to cage the caravan moves,
but I give thanks,

for at each divine juncture
my wings expand
and I

touch Him more
intimately.

YOU HAVE NEVER BEEN LOST

I wanted
to put something on this page that might
make your heart see as
mine,

for the Truth lives in me now;
its ways I
know.

When God flowed into Himself, He made the mill happy.

These words, light ground,
hold them.

Every world sent out its scouts looking
for a merchant who can say,

"You have never been lost dear;
it is God who became
confused."

When He returns home
the mill will
sing.

Existence leans its mouth
toward me,
because my love
cares for
it.

SO FRAGILE AS WE GROW

Someday you will hear all things applaud your wonder.
Life claps in awe of the Divine's performance.
When your veil is removed, you, dear—
you, everyone—will see
that your being is
Holy.

Raising their children is the primary care and purpose
of some—this is a blessed state,
for an oasis of love
is found in the
desert.

The heart only reflects the Sky when it is giving and
compassionate.
Who would want to stand before a mirror that was shattered,
and thus distorts our
beauty

that is so fragile
as we grow.

An oasis
for all life the soul becomes
when it is unveiled.

HOW LONG COULD IT FLIRT?

How long can the moth flirt
near the mouth of the flame before their lips touch
and the moth's soul
becomes like
a sun.

And does the moth then die? No.
In serving God one is transformed into Him.

What lovers would return to us,
what lovers would not unite beyond belief and annihilate
their separation forever if they
had the power
to do so?

That power our Lord has. How long do you think
you can just flirt with Him before you
dissolve in ecstasy?

Existence spins on His potter's wheel;
all is being shaped into the Divine.

What lovers would
not want to die
embraced?

BUT HE WANTED ME

I could not bear to touch God with my own hand
when He came within
my reach,

but He wanted me
to hold
Him.

How God solved my blessed agony,
who can understand?

He turned my
body into
His.

I BET GOD

If He
let go of my hand, I would
weep so loudly,

I would petition with all my might, I would cause
so much trouble

that I bet God would come to His senses
and never do that
again.

LOVE DOES THAT

All day long a little burro labors, sometimes
with heavy loads on her back and sometimes just with worries
about things that bother only
burros.

And worries, as we know, can be more exhausting
than physical labor.

Once in a while a kind monk comes
to her stable and brings
a pear, but more
than that,

he looks into the burro's eyes and touches her ears

and for a few seconds the burro is free
and even seems to laugh,   ·

because love does
that.

Love frees.

THE HOPE OF LOVING

What keeps us alive, what allows us to endure?
I think it is the hope of loving,
or being loved.

I heard a fable once about the sun going on a journey
to find its source, and how the moon wept
without her lover's
warm gaze.

We weep when light does not reach our hearts. We wither
like fields if someone close
does not rain their
kindness
upon
us.

THE SPIRIT'S HANDS

They

can be a great help—words.

They can become the spirit's hands

and lift and

caress

you.

HOW THEN CAN WE ARGUE?

Having lunch in a field one day, I troubled an ant with a
question. I asked of him humbly,

"Have you ever been to Paris?"
And he replied, "No, but I wouldn't mind going." And then he asked me
if I had ever been to a famous ant city. And I regretted that I
hadn't, and was quick to add, "I wouldn't mind, *too!*"

This led to a conclusion: There is life that we do not know of.
How aware are we of all consciousness
in this universe?

What percent of space is this earth in the infinite realm?
What percent of time is one second
in eternity?

Less than that is our
knowledge of

God.

How then can we ever
argue about

Him?

EXPANDS HIS BEING

All beings
are words of God,
His music, His
art.

Sacred books we are, for the infinite camps
in our
souls.

Every act reveals God and expands His Being.
I know that may be hard
to comprehend.

All creatures are doing their best
to help God in His birth
of Himself.

Enough talk for the night.
He is laboring in me;

I need to be silent
for a while,

worlds are forming
in my heart.

A PLAGUE

What a cruel act to be untruthful.
Earthquakes happen in the heart that hears sounds
that are amiss.

Havoc is created in the mind that can no longer trust someone
once loved, and schisms devour alliances
that help support
our life.

Words can enrich and be as wonderful spices mixed into the days
we imbibe with all our senses.

There are fields in the soul—lush organic meadows, though sounds
and words that fall there
can be, at times, a
poison.

A plague is spread by one
who cannot tell
the truth.

EVERYTHING

Everything I see, hear, touch, feel, taste,
speak, think,
imagine,

is completing a perfect circle
God has drawn.

AN INSIDIOUS IDOL

Commerce is supported by keeping the individual at odds
with himself and others, by making us want more than we need, and
offering credit to buy what refined senses do not want.

The masses become shackled; I see how their eyes weep
and are desperate—of course they feel desperate—for something,
for some remedy

that a poor soul then feels *needs*
to be bought.

I find nothing more offensive than a god
who could condemn human instincts in us that time in all its wonder
have made perfect.

I find nothing more destructive to the well-being of life
than to support a god that makes you feel unworthy and in debt to it.
I imagine erecting churches to such a strange god will assure
endless wars that commerce loves.

A god that could frighten is not a god—but an insidious idol
and weapon in the hands of
the insane.

A god who talks of sin is worshipped
by the infirm;

I was once spiritually ill—we all pass through that—
but one day the intelligence
in my soul
cured
me.

AN IMAGE THAT MAKES THEM SAD

How long will grown men and women in this world
keep drawing in their coloring books
an image of God that
makes them
sad?

IT IS A LIE

It is a lie—any talk of God
that does not
comfort
you.

THE PASSION IN HER WHISPER

Only in a dream could this happen:

such terror that I have seen in eyes, and men abusing women,
and cries from the pores
of the sky.

So how to wake the sleeping?

I was once consumed in thought,
trying to make sense of a very unwanted experience,
when a bird's tune called to me from a
nearby limb.

And this brought me understanding, that audience with love,
and the way beauty can let us hold her
in mind and
arms.

The passion in the earth's whisper
grew so loud
I woke.

Now I cannot deny
all is
He.

TO SEE AS GOD SEES

It is your destiny to see as God sees,
to know as God knows,
to feel as God
feels.

How is this possible? How?
Because divine love cannot defy its very self.

Divine love will be eternally true to its own being,
and its being is giving all it can,
at the perfect
moment.

And the greatest gift
God can give is His own experience.

Every object, every creature, every man, woman and child
has a soul and it is the destiny of all,

to see as God sees, to know as God knows,
to feel as God feels, to Be
as God
Is.

St. Thomas Aquinas

Because of my compassion the sun wanted to be near me all night,
and the earth deeded her fields to me, and all in heaven said,

"We have voted you our governor; tell us your divine mandate."
And I did, and God will never revoke it:

Nothing in existence is turned away.

Thomas Aquinas (1225–1274) is widely regarded as the greatest Catholic theologian. One could say he was a spiritual master, always striving to reveal to others the path to Christ. It is said that toward the end of his life he asked Jesus to pass judgment upon one of his books, and Jesus replied: "You have written well; continue to write whatever your heart wishes to express."

Thomas was born in Aquino, Italy, near Naples, into a noble family. At the age of five he was sent to the Benedictine Abbey of Monte Cassino to receive his basic education, in the hope that he would someday become an influential abbot. At an early age he began to develop a great and lasting love of the scriptures, especially the psalms, and at times he revealed what was to become his hallmark by stunning his teachers with profound questions and insights about God. Here he also developed a great love for meditation and solitude, which he later described as the greatest opportunity offered to a human being, a life of contemplation of the wonders of creation and God.

At the age of seventeen he became a Dominican novice in a

mendicant order. This order, which was considered countercultural, had been started by a contemporary of St. Francis of Assisi and was based on the principles of poverty, preaching, and complete faith in God. Not long after this, Thomas's brothers, at the direction of their mother, kidnapped him and imprisoned him for nearly two years within the family castle to force him to disavow his radical mendicant way of life. Refusing various temptations offered to him, he spent his time memorizing the scriptures. Finally, his family relented and allowed him to return to the Dominicans. After further studies in Naples, he was appointed as a master at the University of Paris in 1257. During this time he came to embrace the long suppressed Aristotelian texts on metaphysics. These texts helped develop in him the ability to present the profound in simple terms, while also creating in Thomas a reverence—and almost scientific approach—to every moment of time and every creature and form in existence. His experience became that all in creation were revelations of God's infinite, eternal, expanding Being.

Over the next sixteen years he composed nearly one hundred truly remarkable works. This prolific output is all the more remarkable in light of the numerous stories of Thomas Aquinas often being absorbed in states of enchantment and being completely unconscious of his surroundings or his actions, even to the point of putting inedible items into his mouth at the dining table.

Near the end of his life he had a divine revelation while celebrating mass in the chapel of St. Nicholas in Naples that caused him to state, "I can no longer write, for God has given me such glorious knowledge that all contained in my works are as straw—barely fit to absorb the holy wonders that fall in a stable." Three months later he died.

ON BEHALF OF LOVE

Every truth without exception—no matter
who makes it—is from God.

If a bird got accused of singing too early
in the morning,

if a lute began to magically play on its own
in the square
and the enchanting sounds it made drove a pair of young lovers
into a wild, public display of
passion,

if this lute and bird then got called before the inquisition
and their lives were literally at stake,

could not God walk up and say before the court,

"All acts of beauty are mine, all happen on the behalf of love"?

And while God was there, testifying for our heart's desires,
hopefully the judge would be astute enough
to brave a question,
that could go,

"Dear God, you say all acts of beauty are yours,
surely we can believe that. But what of all actions
we see in this world,

for is there any force in existence greater than the power
of your omnipresent hand?"

And God might have responded, "I like that question,"
adding, "May I ask you one as well?"

And then God would say,

"Have you ever been in a conversation when children entered
the room, and you then ceased speaking because your
wisdom knew they were not old enough
to benefit—to understand?

As exquisite is your world, most everyone in it
is spiritually young.

Spirituality is love, and love never wars with the minute, the day,
one's self and others. Love would rather die
than maim a limb,
a wing.

Dear, anything that divides man from man,
earth from sky, light and dark, one religion from another . . .
O, I best keep silent, I see a child
just entered the
room."

CLOSE TO GOD

One may never have heard the sacred word "Christ,"
but be closer to God
than a priest or
nun.

FROM MY BREATH

From my breath I extract God.
And my eye is a shop
where I offer
Him to the
world.

THE MANDATE

Because of my compassion, the sun wanted to be near me all night,
and the earth deeded her fields to me,
and all in heaven said,

"We have voted you our governor; tell us your divine mandate."
And I did, and God will never revoke it:

Nothing in existence is turned
away.

More tender is my Lord's heart than any heart
has ever been.

So, when the divine realm asked me to govern it
with one simple
rule,

I looked into His eyes and then knew
what to say to any angel
who might serve as
a sentry to
God:

No creature should be
turned away.

EVERY FOOT A SHRINE

Every creature has a religion. Every
foot is a shrine where
a secret candle
burns.

Every cell in us worships
God.

Every arrow in the bow of desire
has rushed out in hope
of nearing
Him.

WE ARE FIELDS BEFORE EACH OTHER

How is it they live for eons in such harmony—
the billions of stars—

when most men can barely go a minute
without declaring war in their mind against someone they know.

There are wars where no one marches with a flag,
though that does not keep casualties
from mounting.

Our hearts irrigate this earth.
We are fields before
each other.

How can we live in harmony?
First we need to
know

we are all madly in love
with the same
God.

HIS CHOIR

Sing, my tongue; sing, my hand;
sing, my feet, my knee,
my loins, my
whole body.

Indeed I am His
choir.

ASK ANYTHING

"Ask anything,"

My Lord said to me.

And my mind and heart thought deeply
for a second,

then replied with just one word,

"When?"

God's arms then opened up and I entered Myself.
I entered Myself when I entered
Christ.

And having learned compassion I
allowed my soul

to stay.

WHENEVER HE LOOKS AT YOU

God sees nothing in us that He has not given.
Everything is empty until He places
what He wishes into it.

The soul is like an uninhabited world
that comes to life only when
God lays His head
against us.

The delight a child can know
tossing a ball into
the air,

my Lord confessed He experiences
whenever He looks
at you.

God sees nothing in us
that He has not
given.

THE DIVINE INTIMACY

The experience of something out of nothing—
is that not how one might describe magic?

A hat held upside down may appear empty,
though at God's command all life that any planet
has ever known could dance around
the hat's rim, holding
hands.

The root that needs no ground is He,
and from that root all has
come.

Creation is God's litter, and all are
nursed; some grow more plump than others,
indeed.

Eternally amazed is the soul before God,
watching Him expand.

Witnessing God reveal Himself to Himself—
that divine intimacy
I know.

CAPAX UNIVERSI

Capax universi, capable of the universe are your arms
when they move with love.

And I know it is true that your feet are never
more alive than when they are in
defense of a good
cause.

I want to fund your efforts: Stay near beauty, for she will always
strengthen you.

She will bring your mouth close to hers and
breathe—inspire you the way
light does the
fields.

The earth inhales God, why
should we not do
the same?

This sacred flame we tend inside needs
the chants of every tongue,
the communion with
all.

As capable as God
are we.

DOES GOD UNDERSTAND HIMSELF?

Does God understand Himself? Not in the form of creation.

For creation simultaneously exists and does not exist.
How could that not be in a mind that is Infinite?
Thus God holds no one accountable—
especially Himself—at all.

If you had a dream in which someone broke into
your house and stole a certain object,

would you, upon waking and finding that item still there,
call the constable?

Not if you were in your right mind.
And whenever Gods wakes in us

His/our thinking becomes clear—
nothing is missing.

And how could He not forgive, then,
what never really
happened,

and/or—what He
caused?

COULD YOU EMBRACE THAT?

I said to God, "Let me love you."
And He replied, "Which part?"

"All of you, all of you," I said.

"Dear," God spoke, "you are as a mouse wanting to impregnate
a tiger who is not even in heat. It is a feat way
beyond your courage and strength.
You would run from me
if I removed my
mask."

I said to God again,

"Beloved I need to love you—every aspect, every pore."

And this time God said,

"There is a hideous blemish on my body,
though it is such an infinitesimal part of my Being—
could you kiss that if it were revealed?"

"I will try, Lord, I will try."

And then God said,
"That blemish is all the hatred and
cruelty in this
world."

DUCKING

More significant than any act is the power,
the impetus behind it.

An ocean fish may gather enough momentum to leap
into the air and may even fall into a boat
and bite someone;

but tracing that act to its source reveals the Ocean
as the cause.

Our thoughts leap out of God;
creation took flight from His bow.

Behind every act is the Beloved, He is the cause.
The child blames others for their woes.

No one can change the course of His arrows.
That does not mean that one should
not become adept at
ducking.

ON THE SABBATH

On the Sabbath try and make no noise that
goes beyond your
house.

Cries of passion between lovers
are exempt.

WHAT DOES LIGHT TALK ABOUT?

When you recognize her beauty,
the eye applauds, the heart stands in an ovation,

and the tongue when she is near
is on its best behavior,

it speaks more like light.

What does light talk about?
I asked a plant that once.

It said, "I am not sure,
but it makes me
grow."

ZEAL

Zeal,

where does it come from?

I don't have all the answers, but every time His lips touch mine

I get wonderfully

crazy.

THE PULSE OF GOD

The limbs of a tree reached down and lifted me,
thinking I was its
child.

And in the
meadows my spirit becomes so quiet
that if I put my cheek against the earth's body
I feel the pulse of
God.

"Tell me the way you do that, birds—
enter the private chambers of my Lord."

And they all sang,
they just
sang.

I gathered it was time to become a musician,
and I did.

Years passed,
and the sky reached down one day and lifted me;
the birds noticed and
spoke,

"How do you enter the Sun like that
and know the pulse of
God?"

BEAUTY HONES

So many tears behind these words.
Love hones like that—
perfects and
purifies
the
gift.

IF IT HAD NOT BELIEVED

Would any seed take root if it had not believed
His promise, when God said,

"Dears, I will rain. I will help you. I will turn into
warmth and effulgence,

I will be the Mother I am
and let you draw from
My body

and rise, and
rise."

OTHERWISE THE DARKNESS

I
have a cause.
We need those don't we?
Otherwise the darkness and the cold gets in
and everything starts to
ache.

My soul has a purpose, it is
to love;

if I
do not fulfill
my heart's vocation,
I suffer.

ALL THINGS DESIRE

All things desire to be like God,
and infinite space is a mirror
that tries
to reflect His
body.

But it can't.
All that infinite existence can show us of Him
is only an atom of God's
being.

God stood behind Himself one night and cast a
brilliant shadow from which creation
came.

Even this shadow is such a flame that
moths consume their selves in it every second—
with their sacred passion to possess
beautiful
forms.

Existence mirrors God the best it can,
though how arrogant for any image in that mirror,
for any human being, to
think they know
His will;

for His will has never been spoken,
His voice would ignite
the earth's wings

and all upon
it.

We invent truths about God to protect ourselves
from the wolf's cries we hear
and make.

All things desire to be like God,
all things desire to
love.

YOU CANNOT BE WHAT GOD IS NOT

All are having a relationship with God.
A pear taken from a limb and
set in a bowl,

surely it is talking to its Lord,
and happy that it is being honored for its life,

and somehow knowing
that soon it will be
returning to
Him.

We use words like "returning."
Think about that. Inherent in that word is
separation,

and separation from God is never
really possible.

What can you be that He is not? "You
cannot be what I am not,"
my Lord once said
to me.

GOD'S NATURE

Sometimes we think what we are saying about God
is true when in fact
it is not.

It would seem of value to differentiate between what is
God's nature and what is false about Love.

I have come to learn that the truth never harms
or frightens.

I have come to learn that
God's compassion and light can never be limited;

thus any God who could condemn is
not a god at all

but some disturbing image in the
mind of a
child

we best ignore, until we
can cure the
dark.

THE CHRIST SAID

The
Christ said to us,
"I have cut you from a garden I tend
and set you in a vase
for the world
to see.

Soon you will return, for your glorious presence I miss.

My hands need to touch you again, my
divine senses and eyes require
your soul's beauty
near.

Forgive me, my love, for the suffering
our separation
brought.

If I said I am in debt to you,
could you

understand?"

Hafiz

God revealed a sublime truth to the world when He sang, "I am made whole by your life. Each soul, each soul completes me."

Shams-ud-din Muhammad Hafiz (c.1320–1389) is the most beloved poet of Persians and is considered to be one of history's greatest lyrical geniuses. Though he is still little known in the Western world, many notables including Emerson, Goethe, García Lorca, the composer Brahms and even Nietzsche were deeply affected by him. Emerson once remarked that "Hafiz is a poet for poets," and Goethe wrote that "Hafiz has no peer." The range of Hafiz's work is astounding, striking a chord of recognition in people from every stratum of mind.

Hafiz was born Shams-ud-din Muhammad, the youngest of three sons, in the beautiful garden city of Shiraz in southern Persia, where he remained most of his life. Shiraz escaped the ravages of the Tartar and Mongol invasions during this violent and chaotic time, and Persian life as Hafiz knew it as a child and young adult was for the most part wonderful and steeped in nature's poetry. And Hafiz's father undoubtedly recited the verse of Saadi, Farid-ud-din Attar, and Jalal-ud-din Rumi to his sons as well as the Quran. In fact, Shams-ud-din Muhammad later chose the pen name of Hafiz, which means "memorizer" and denotes a person who knows the entire Quran by heart.

When Hafiz was in his teens, his father, who had been a coal merchant, died. Hafiz began working as a baker's assistant to help support the family, and at night attended school, eventually obtaining a "classical" medieval education. A famous story about Hafiz, told many ways, says: When he was twenty-one he was delivering bread to a wealthy noble family and glimpsed a remarkably beautiful girl on a terrace of the home. He fell desperately in love with her, but she had already been promised to another. Still, he began writing and singing out poems for her that expressed his longing and adoration. The poems were so touching that many in Shiraz came to know of them, and they were sung to other's sweethearts. Out of desperation to win her, Hafiz undertook a forty-night vigil at the tomb of a famous saint, for legend had it that anyone who could accomplish this feat would win their heart's desire. Indeed, after a Herculean effort, upon completion of the fortieth night of vigil, it is said the archangel Gabriel appeared before Hafiz and asked him what he desired. Gazing upon the radiant beauty of God's angel, Hafiz forgot his human love, and the thought rushed into his mind: "What must God's beauty be like—my soul needs to see that, I need to see God." Gabriel then revealed to him the whereabouts of a spiritual teacher in Shiraz whom, if served faithfully, would bring about the fulfillment of his wish. This teacher was Muhammad Attar, who lived a seemingly ordinary life to the world's eyes—that of a chemist or perfumer with a shop in Shiraz. Few knew of his secret status as a great spiritual master.

Attar guided Hafiz in the development of his poetry and in the unfolding of his soul. It is said that Hafiz's poems contain and reveal all the stages of divine vision, experience, and love. He cloaked all these truths in vernacular garb, as was the tradition in Sufi schools at that time, since secrecy was often essential in the climate of life-threatening fundamentalism.

During the next decade of his life Hafiz gained much fame and influence as a poet, obtaining court patronage and a teaching position at a college that may have even been founded for him. In his early thirties an opposing sect ruled Shiraz and Hafiz was dismissed from the college. It is thought that he probably fell back upon his skill as a copyist as he had mastered the art of calligraphy during his educational training. Some years later he was reinstated. In his early forties he again fell out of favor with the ruling court as his poems were often very controversial and he even more so; eventually Hafiz had to flee Shiraz for his safety. After several years he was able to return.

When Hafiz was about sixty, it is believed that his beloved master, Muhammad Attar, granted Hafiz his deepest most constant desire—union with God. Hafiz's forty-year spiritual consecration bequeathed to history some of the most profound mystical verse in print. An estimated 5,000 poems were written by Hafiz throughout his life though it is a tremendous loss that not one poem remains in his own handwriting and the authenticity of anything tagged Hafiz will always be an issue that concerns scholars. Let the gauge of authenticity be courageous and true, like these words attributed to Hafiz: "No one could ever paint a too wonderful picture of my heart or God."

It is said of Hafiz that he wrote with a sweet, playful genius unparalleled in world literature. He is rightfully called "The Tongue of the Invisible," for through his works he continues to sing beautiful and wild love songs to this world from God.

THE CHRIST'S BREATH

I am
a hole in a flute
that the Christ's breath moves through—
listen to this
music.

OUR UNION

Our
union is like this:

You feel cold so I reach for a blanket to cover
our shivering feet.

A hunger comes into your body
so I run to my garden and start digging potatoes.

You asked for a few words of comfort and guidance and
I quickly kneel by your side offering you
a whole book as a
gift.

You ache with loneliness one night so much
you weep, and I say

here is a rope, tie it around me,
Hafiz will be your
companion for
life.

STARTLED BY GOD

Not like

a lone beautiful bird

these poems now rise in great white flocks

startled by God breaking a branch

when His foot touches

earth near

me.

POSITIONS OF LOVE

There are so many positions of love:
each curve on a
branch,

the thousand ways your eyes can hold us,
the infinite shapes each mind
can draw,

the spring orchestra of scents and sounds wafting through the air,
the currents of light combusting like
passionate
lips,

the revolution of the universe's skirt, whose folds
contain other worlds,

our every sigh that falls against
His inconceivably close,
omnipresent,
divine
body.

LOUSY AT MATH

Once a group of thieves stole a rare diamond
larger than two goose eggs.

Its value could have easily bought three thousand horses
and three thousand acres of the most
fertile land in
Shiraz.

The thieves got drunk that night to celebrate their great haul,
but during the course of the evening the effects of the liquor,
and their mistrust of each other grew
to such an extent

they decided to divide the stone into pieces.
Of course then the Priceless became lost.

Most everyone is lousy at math and does that to God—
dissects the Indivisible One,

by thinking, by saying,
"This is my Beloved, he looks like this and acts like that,
how could that moron over there
really
be

God?"

IF GOD INVITED YOU TO A PARTY

If God
invited you to a party and
said,

"Everyone in the ballroom tonight will
be my special
guest,"

how would you then treat them when you arrived?

Indeed, indeed!

And Hafiz knows that there is no one in
this world who is not standing upon

His jeweled dance
floor.

I HAVE COME INTO THIS WORLD TO SEE THIS

I have come into this world to see this:
the sword drop from men's hands even at the height
of their arc of anger

because we have finally realized there is just one flesh to wound
and it is His—the Christ's, our
Beloved's.

I have come into this world to see this: all creatures hold hands as
we pass through this miraculous existence we share on the way
to even a greater being of soul,

a being of just ecstatic light, forever entwined and at play
with Him.

I have come into this world to hear this:

every song the earth has sung since it was conceived in
the Divine's womb and began spinning from
His wish,

every song by wing and fin and hoof,
every song by hill and field and tree and woman and child,
every song of stream and rock,

every song of tool and lyre and flute,
every song of gold and emerald
and fire,

every song the heart should cry with magnificent dignity
to know itself as
God;

for all other knowledge will leave us again in want and aching—
only imbibing the glorious Sun
will complete us.

I have come into the world to experience this:

men so true to love
they would rather die before speaking
an unkind
word,

men so true their lives are His covenant—
the promise of
hope.

I have come into this world to see this:
the sword drop from men's hands
even at the height of
their arc of
rage

because we have finally realized
there is just one flesh

we can wound.

HOW DID THE ROSE?

How

did the rose

ever open its heart

and give to this world all of its beauty?

It felt the encouragement of light against its being,

otherwise we all remain too

frightened.

POWER IS SAFEST IN A POET'S HANDS

Power is safest in a poet's hands, thus for the artist
God will
pose.

The realms of thought sublimely wild, the finest pigments of
ground suns, the violin's divine plea for a
true friend;

what is all this world has seen from art: the shadow more true and
glorious there

than in the cage where there is often talk of right and wrong.

The reins of God say to His lover,

"Hold me in your mouth, dear,
as you toil with all your limbs and strength
to free the magnificence
in man."

The reins of the Sky sing,

"Grab hold, and you will know God
lowers His cup into you
to drink."

THE WOMAN I LOVE

Because the Woman I love lives inside of you,

I lean as close to your body with my words as I can—
and I think of you all the time,
dear pilgrim.

Because the One I love goes with you wherever you go,
Hafiz will always be
near.

If you sat before me, wayfarer, with your aura bright from
your many charms,

my lips could resist rushing to you, but my eyes, my eyes
can no longer hide the wondrous fact of who
you really are.

The Beautiful One whom I adore
has pitched His royal tent inside of you,

so I will always lean my heart
as close to your soul
as I can.

THE TRUE NATURE OF YOUR BELOVED

Know
the true nature of your
Beloved.

In
His
loving eyes
your every thought, word, and movement
is always, always

beautiful.

ONLY PUCKER AT CERTAIN MOMENTS?

Does God only pucker at certain moments
of one's life?

No way!

He is the wildest of us
lovers.

PERFECT EQUANIMITY

Look how a mirror
will reflect with perfect equanimity
all actions
before
it.

There is no act in this world
that will ever cause the mirror to look away.
There is no act in this world that will
ever make the mirror
say "no."

The mirror, like perfect love, will just keep giving
of itself to all
before
it.

How did the mirror ever get like that, so polite,
so grand, so compassionate?

It watched God.

Yes, the mirror remembers the Beloved
looking into itself as the Beloved shaped existence's heart
and the mirror's
soul.

My eye has the nature of God.
Hafiz looks upon all with perfect equanimity,
as do my words,
dear.

My poems will never tell you no,
because the Mirror is
not like
that,

and if God ever hits you with a don't—
He has His fingers crossed,

He is just fibbing
for your own
good.

TROUBLED?

Troubled?
Then stay with me, for I am not.

Lonely?
A thousand naked amorous ones dwell in ancient caves
beneath my eyelids.

Riches?
Here's a pick,
my whole body is an emerald that begs,
"Take me."

Write all that worries you on a piece of parchment;
offer it to God.
Even from the distance of a millennium

I can lean the flame in my heart
into your life

and turn
all that frightens you
into holy
incense
ash.

TINY GODS

Some
gods say, the tiny ones,
"I am not here in your vibrant, moist lips
that need to beach themselves upon the golden shore
of a naked body."

Some gods say, "I am not the scarred yearning in the unrequited soul;
I am not the blushing cheek of every star and planet—

I am not the applauding Creator of those precious secretions that
can distill the whole mind into a perfect wincing jewel
if only for a moment;

nor do I reside in every pile of sweet warm dung born
of the earth's gratuity."

Some gods say, the ones we need to hang,
"Your mouth is not designed to know His, love was not conceived
to consume the luminous realms."

Dear ones beware,
beware of the tiny gods frightened men
worship

to bring an anesthetic control and relief
to their sad
days.

THE SUN NEVER SAYS

Even
after
all this time
the sun never says to the earth,

"You owe me."

Look
what happens
with a love like that—

it lights the whole
world.

TWO GIANT FAT PEOPLE

God

and I have become

like two giant fat people living

in a tiny

boat.

We

keep bumping into

each other

and

l
a
u
g
h
i
n
g
.

ONE REGRET

One regret that I am determined not to have
when I am lying upon my
death bed

is that we did not kiss
enough.

AND SHE WROTE POEMS

Quietly
her fame spread,
that courtesan who few had heard of
a year
ago.

Shy men could do with her what they could
with no one
else.

And women
too sought her breasts
and came to know how wonderful touch
could be.

And
she wrote poems
and left her eyes there for they were
what loved the
most.

BEAUTIFUL CREATURE

There is a beautiful creature living
in a hole you have
dug,

so at night I set fruit and grains and little pots of wine and milk
beside your soft earthen
mounds,

and I often sing to you,
but still, my dear, you do not come out.

I have fallen in love with someone
who is hiding inside
of you.

We should talk about this problem,
otherwise I will never
leave you
alone!

WITH THAT MOON LANGUAGE

Admit something:

Everyone you see, you say to them, "Love me."

Of course you do not do this out loud, otherwise
someone would call the cops.

Still, though, think about this, this great pull in us to connect.

Why not become the one who lives with a
full moon in each eye that is
always saying,

with that sweet moon language,
what every other eye in
this world is
dying to
hear?

JUST SIT THERE RIGHT NOW

Just
sit there right now.
Don't do a thing. Just rest.

For your
separation from God
is the hardest work in this world.

Let me bring you trays of food and something
that you like to
drink.

You can use my soft words
as a cushion
for your
head.

WONDROUS

O wondrous creatures,

by what strange miracle do you

so often not

smile?

MY SWEET, CRUSHED ANGEL

You have
not danced so badly, my dear,
trying to hold hands with the Beautiful One.

You have waltzed with great style, my sweet, crushed angel,
to have ever neared God's heart at all.

Our Partner is notoriously difficult to follow, and even His
best musicians are not always easy to hear.

So what if the music has stopped for a while.
So what if the price of admission to the Divine is out of reach tonight.

So what, my sweetheart, if you lack the ante to gamble for real love.

The mind and the body are famous for holding the heart ransom,
but Hafiz knows the Beloved's eternal habits. Have patience,
for He will not be able to resist your longings
and charms for long.

You have not danced so badly, my dear,
trying to kiss the Magnificent
One.

You have actually waltzed with tremendous style,
my sweet, O my sweet,
crushed
angel.

EACH SOUL COMPLETES ME

My
Beloved said,

"My name is not complete without
yours."

I thought:
How could a human's worth ever be such?

And God, knowing all our thoughts—and all our
thoughts are innocent steps on the path—
then addressed my
heart,

God revealed
a sublime truth to the world,
when He
sang,

"I am made whole by your life. Each soul,
each soul completes
me."

St. Catherine of Siena

If I did not understand the glory and sufferings of the human heart
I would not speak before its holiness.

St. Catherine (1347–1380) was said to have been profoundly interested in every human being that ever came before her. She devoted herself to relieving the mental and emotional suffering of the hundreds who sought her out; her words and her touch bestowed a soothing grace. "Strange," she once said, "that so much suffering is caused because of the misunderstanding of God's true nature. God's heart is more gentle than the Virgin's first kiss upon the Christ. And God's forgiveness to all, to any thought or act, is more certain than our own being."

Catherine Benincasa was born March 25, 1347, in the Fontebranda district of Siena, Italy. She and her twin sister, who died soon after birth, were two of more than twenty children born to parents who were devout Catholics. It was a time of class feuds and religious wars as well as the Black Plague and famine in Siena; it was the time of transition from the Middle Ages to the Renaissance.

One day when Catherine was six years old, she and her brother were returning from her older sister's house; as they neared the church of the Dominican friars, set upon the beautiful hill of Campporeggi, Catherine looked up above the church and saw in the sunset Jesus and three of his apostles. Jesus smiled at her and raised his hand in a blessing. Catherine became happy beyond any delight she had ever known. She became transfixed by this vision, and it took her brother's tugging at her arm to bring her back into this world. She was transformed by this experience and began devoting her life to finding God through solitude, fasting, and prayer.

When Catherine was seven years old her longing to wed God became so intense she left home alone to find a cave in the forest of Leccto where a known settlement of hermits was said to live. Taking with her only a loaf of bread, she soon found herself in the enchanting hillside forest. To her great surprise and delight she discovered a cave that she thought was a perfect place in which to spend her life seeking God. During the night, while in prayer, Catherine felt a great uneasiness come over her body, and her limbs became numb. Feeling a little frightened, suddenly she heard a divine voice say, "How brave you are my child, but let our wedding be later." The next thing Catherine knew she was at home in her own bed, no one had missed her, and she was absolutely sure that what had happened was not a dream. The next day she took her brother to the cave and asked him to go inside and see if anything was there. He returned, carrying two sticks Catherine had bound together into a little cross with part of the hem torn from her dress and also the uneaten loaf of bread. She had leaned this cross upright against the east wall and had also placed the bread there, intending to fast as long as she could. On seeing these, Catherine fell upon her knees with deep thanks and happiness and a faith in God.

As she became older, she resisted her parents' pressure to marry, and became a Dominican nun. At twenty-one she returned to her family to begin a life of active service to the infirm and destitute, while maintaining a deep interior life of contemplation. Jesus appeared to her many times, sometimes performing miracles, and nourishing her deep love for Him. She was a diplomat and people from all walks of life sought her counsel.

St. Catherine died at the age of thirty-three. She was a rare, fearless human being whose faith in God turned into tangible experiences with the Divine. Although she thought of herself as uneducated, her book, *The Dialogue* and her other writings are highly valued by theologians. She had no official appointment, yet it is clear she served as the Church's conscience. In 1970, Pope Paul VI proclaimed her a "Doctor of the Church."

CONSUMED IN GRACE

I first saw God when I was a child, six years of age.
The cheeks of the sun were pale before Him,
and the earth acted as a shy
girl, like me.

Divine light entered my heart from His love
that did never fully wane,

though indeed, dear, I can understand how a person's
faith can at times flicker,

for what is the mind to do
with something that becomes the mind's ruin:
a God that consumes us
in His grace.

I have seen what you want;
it is there,

a Beloved of infinite
tenderness.

LIVE WITHOUT THOUGHT OF DYING

We work so hard to fly
and no matter what heights we reach
our wings get folded near a candle,
at the end,

for nothing can enter God but Himself.
Our souls are some glorious substance of the divine
that no sentry wants to stop.

Live without thought of dying,
for dying is not a truth.

We have swayed on the sky's limb together,
many years there the same leaves grow.

But then they get that look in their eyes
and bid farewell to what they disdained or cherished.

This life He gave the shell, the daily struggles we know,
sit quiet for a minute, dear, feel the wind,
let Light touch you.

Live without thought of dying,
for dying is not a
truth.

VULNERABLE

Vulnerable we are, like an infant.
We need each other's care
or we will
suffer.

I WON'T TAKE NO FOR AN ANSWER

"I won't take no for an answer,"
God began to say
to me

when He opened His arms each night
wanting us to
dance.

THEY KISS SOMETIMES

They kiss sometimes when no one is looking,
the sun and
moon.

Why are they so shy before us—
haven't we all seen someone making love?

I wept once for three days because He
would not touch
me—

for is it not a bride's right
to know Him?

I have seen what I want in heaven's shop.
Crazed I have become for this.

He was sitting in a window one day, my Lord,
when I walked through the sky's
streets.

NO ONE WILL BEGRUDGE ME

I talk about it sometimes with Him, all the suffering in the world.

"Dear God," I have prayed, "how is it possible
all the horrors I have seen, all the atrocities you allow man
to commit when you—God—are ever standing
so near and could help us?
Could we not hear your voice say 'No'
with such love and power
never again would
we harm?"

And my Lord replied, "Who would understand if I said that I
cannot bear
to confine a wing, and not let it learn from the course it chooses."

But what of a man walking lost in a forest
weeping and calling your name for help, and unknown to him he
is heading for a covered pit with sharp spears in it
that will maim his flesh when he crashes
through the trap?

"Yes, why don't I remove every object from this world that could
cause someone to weep? Yes, why don't I speak in a way
that could save a life?

I opened up my hand and the Infinite ran to the edges of space—
and all possibilities are contained therein, all possibilities,
even sorrow.

In the end, nothing that ever caused one pain will exist.
No one will begrudge me.

The Absolute Innocence of all within my creation
takes a while to understand."

THAT SKILL

A thorn has entered your foot. That is why you
weep at times at
night.

There are some in this world
who can pull it
out.

The skill that takes they have
learned from
Him.

WHEREVER YOU MAY LOOK

Wisdom is
so kind and wise
that wherever you may look
you can learn something
about God.

Why
would not
the omnipresent
teach that
way?

NOTHING MAKES MORE SENSE

The force that created the unimaginable splendors
and the unimaginable horrors
has taken refuge
in us,

and it will follow our
commands.

Power in the hands of the weak creates suffering
and divides men.

Those who have held beauty work to overcome their prejudice
and seek to bring all into
Her arms,

for nothing makes more sense
than being there
with Him.

THIS PLACE OF ABUNDANCE

We know nothing until we know everything.

I have no object to defend
for all is of equal value
to me.

I cannot lose anything in this
place of abundance
I found.

If something my heart cherishes
is taken away,

I just say, "Lord, what
happened?"

And a hundred more
appear.

IF SOMEONE CRIED IN HEAVEN

If you cried in heaven, everyone
would laugh

for they would know you were just
kidding.

REST IN PRAYER

The sun hears the fields talking about effort
and the sun
smiles,

and whispers to
me,

"Why don't the fields just rest, for
I am willing to do
everything

to help them
grow?"

Rest, my dears, in
prayer.

THE FOUNDATION OF GOD

My perfect Lord sang,

"Less likely is God to condemn my hand's action
than condemn any
soul."

How could that be possible,
my heart thought?

And the Christ, knowing all minds, replied,

"Forgiveness is the foundation of God's
being."

TO EVEN DRESS

A great helplessness I felt at times
to even dress myself some days,

so I prayed with all my heart,
"Dear God, help me."

It is not possible for Love
to not hear
us,

and whatever happens
the perfect teacher
staged.

What would a wise, powerful king allow
a beloved child to see?

THE HYMNS OF THE EARTH

I wanted to be a hermit and only hear the hymns
of the earth, and the laughter of the sky,

and the sweet gossip of the creatures on my limbs,
the forests.

I wanted to be a hermit and not see another face
look upon mine and tell me I was not
all the beauty in this
world.

For so many faces do that—
cage us.

The wings we have are so fragile
they can break from just
one word, or

a glance void
of love.

I wanted to live in that cloister of
light's silence

because, is it not true, the heart
is so fragile and shy.

CONSECRATED

All has been consecrated.
The creatures in the forest know this,

the earth does, the seas do, the clouds know
as does the heart full of
love.

Strange a priest would rob us of this
knowledge

and then empower himself
with the ability

to make holy what
already was.

HIS LIPS UPON THE VEIL

He has never left you.

It is just
that your soul is so vast
that just like

the earth in its innocence,
it may think,

"I do not feel my lover's warmth
against my face right
now."

But look, dear,
is not the sun reaching down its arms
and always holding a continent
in its light?

God cannot leave us.
It is just that our soul is so vast,

we do not always feel His lips
upon the
veil.

GIVE THE HEART MORE STRENGTH

Herbs can help the body and give
the heart more strength
to love.

When my sight became clearer,
I could see auras around different foods,

and I now know—should I say this?—
that everything can sing.

The songs of fruits and grains will calm,
why not put them into yourself,
a new language you
will learn.

And just touching life's requirements
close to their source
will add grace to your
movements.

More generous eyes we need.
The songs of light
will help
you.

SMELLS OF GOOD FOOD

Truth never frightens.
I remember once walking out in the winter
to greet my father as he returned from work.

He was a little late that night
and I waited by a street corner near our house.

The cold can enliven thanks, my wool coat
became a sacred robe, how happy I felt to be alive.

I waited in a world of magic,
smells of good food,
the street lamps, the smoke coming from chimneys,
the candles burning in windows,
the snow.

Angels feasted, as I did, on existence and God kept saying,
"Have more of what I made."

I saw him coming. We ran into each other's arms
and he lifted me as he so often had—
twirled me through the air,
his hands beneath
my arms.

That is what the Truth does:
lifts and lets us
fly.

YOUR HAIR, YOUR FACE

What is it
you want to change?
Your hair, your face, your body?
Why?

For God is
in love with all those things
and He might weep
when they are
gone.

ONLY IF YOU JOIN ME

One more song tonight, okay, but only
if you join me.

Once, when I was sad, I said to a kind old priest,
"Have you learned any secrets
to unburden the
heart?"

And he responded,

"Hum a favorite melody;
wine will always rise
to the top
of oil."

THE SANCTUARY

It could be said that God's foot is so vast
that this entire earth is but a
field on His
toe,

and all the forests in this world
came from the same root of just
a single hair
of His.

What then is not a sanctuary?
Where then can I not kneel
and pray at a shrine
made holy by His
presence?

WHEN SOMEONE I LOVE IS NEAR

I know the vows the sun and moon took;
they are in love but they don't
touch.

But why should I not let my face become
lit before this
earth

when someone I cherish
is near?

A PEASANT BEFORE A KING

If I did not understand
the glory and sufferings of the human heart,
I would not speak before its
holiness.

Like a peasant called before a great king,
when all of His court is assembled—

that is how I stand before
every woman and
man.

How is it that God seeks our counsel
whenever a voice or face
asks of us?

What a sweet divine game
He plays.

I stand with humility before every creature
when they call me into
their court,

because of your holiness,
my dears.

UNTIL YOUR OWN DAWN

Daybreak:
everything in this world is a luminous divine dream
I have spun.

I did not know life was a fabric woven by my soul.
Any form that can appear to you—should I confess this?—
it is something I made.
All roots nurse
from
me.

God's art is mine. I did not want His divine talent.
It simply grew in my heart from
the way I
loved.

Existence is as a young child moving through
a lane at night;

it wanted to
hold my
hand.

Here, dear earth, hold me,
until your own
dawn.

Kabir

The fish in the water that is thirsty needs
serious professional counseling.

For five hundred years the poems of Kabir (c.1440–1518) have been recited and sung throughout India. Kabir was a great religious reformer in his time, as well as a famous artist and musician, founding a sect that still claims to have a million followers. Kabir achieved a remarkable synthesis of Hindu, Muslim, and even Christian belief. Rabindranath Tagore, the famous Bengali poet and novelist who won the Noble Prize for Literature in 1913, was a major force in bringing the wonderful poems of Kabir to the attention of the West when he published some translations of Kabir in 1915.

Some present-day readers of Kabir liken him to something of a tough guy, a Zen-bruiser, a divine smart-aleck, but there are many dimensions of this great Master that one can bring to light, including his rarely revealed tenderness and his delicious freeing humor. As all of Kabir's poems were—probably—originally songs, one of the many legends surrounding his life may be true: he chose not to read or write, as this rendering also leads one to think:

Paper would turn to flame if I touched it in an ecstatic mood.
And ink dries if it comes a hundred feet within
the radiance of one who will not let God
leave their arms.

Why trouble a pen to labor,
I've got naked angels camping on my floors with nothing more to
do than imprint my words upon the sky when I sing them.

Having mentioned the fate of paper when I am in love, and I am
always in love, how could a sun like me ever appear dressed?

Sounds like an interesting mystery that can help the bored
pass some time.

Kabir was born in Varanasi, in North India, into a family of weavers who had recently converted to Islam, though it is widely believed that he was a disciple of a famous Hindu guru, Ramananda.

While a family man and a weaver, Kabir passionately sought to show the way out of delusion, including the delusion of religious identity. During his lifetime both mainstream Hindus and Muslims denounced him, only coming to claim and revere him as their own after his death. Kabir was well aware of the misunderstanding of the public toward a true mystic. This is reflected in the unique irony that pervades his poetry. Even so there can be discovered a remarkable compassion and tenderness in his verse, as portrayed in "No Harm Done."

Kabir's life both exemplifies and parallels all of the saints in this book, as well as any living Master. That is, saints will usually create or allow controversy about themselves that then serves as a kind of watchdog to keep the world at an arm's distance. The people who can get close to such a saint have to go through an ego-dying process. It is a paradoxical spiritual truth: The closer a teacher is to God the harder they are to have faith in and/or live around while the less advanced the teacher is the more they can be easily accepted by the average person. Kabir, even when he had many wealthy followers, chose to live in a very small rundown house in a rough section of town where people were afraid to venture at night. It was the same area where the butchers had their shops, where the dying shrieks of animals confronted all ears, and where the stench of slaughtered animals could become unbearable in the summer months. The circumstances Kabir lived in were especially challenging to some of his Hindu disciples who were strict vegetarians. Where he chose to live would probably have kept many of his present-day readers so at odds with their spiritual standards that they would not even visit Kabir if he were alive today. My point being that what we see of historic saints is often tremendously edited, as the way a parent might edit what their child hears and sees. Christianity as a whole at times strikes me as a remarkably edited view of God, as do the beliefs of any religion that promotes any kind of division between the soul and creation; but how wonderful such views exist to help the spiritually young grow. The problem though becomes: we begin to want God on our terms not His. And our conditional terms will probably always keep us separate from the One we say we love and the One we need to unite with; what an irony.

With so much religious propaganda playing havoc with us, when I felt it was legitimate I have tried to fill in some of the blanks—un-edit light's freedom—and not weaken the sweet divine punches like this playful, witty one—again—when Kabir says:

The fish in the water that is thirsty needs
serious professional counseling.

The glorious role of the mystical poets is to help us accept God more as He Is—and ever less than our prejudices and fears want Him to be.

May Kabir's poems help reduce the income of psychiatrists, and maybe even undermine a military budget or two. Why not dream big?

I JUST LAUGH

If I told you the truth about God,
you might think I was an
idiot.

If I lied to you about the Beautiful One
you might parade me through the streets shouting,
"This guy is a genius!"

This world has its pants on backwards.
Most carry their values and knowledge in a jug
that has a big hole in it.

Thus having a clear grasp of the situation
if I am asked anything these days

I just laugh!

WHAT KIND OF GOD?

What kind of God would He be
if He did not hear the
bangles ring on
an ant's
wrist

as they move the earth
in their sweet
dance?

And what kind of God would He be
if a leaf's prayer was not as precious to creation
as the prayer His own son sang
from the glorious depth
of his soul—
for us.

And what kind of God would He be
if the vote of millions in this world could sway Him
to change the divine
law of
love

that speaks so clearly with compassion's elegant tongue,
saying, eternally saying:

all are forgiven—moreover, dears,
no one has ever been
guilty.

What
kind of God would He be
if He did not count the blinks
of your
eyes

and is in absolute awe of their movements?

What a God—what a God we
have.

THE SMART DOGS RAN OFF

I sat one day with a priest who expounded on the
doctrine of hell.

I listened to him for hours, then he asked me
what I thought of all
he said.

And I replied,

"That doctrine seems an inhumane cage;
no wonder the smart dogs
ran off."

A MAN WITH AMNESIA

With a begging bowl in hand a man with amnesia knocks
on his own door.

My guru cured me of that profound illness:

God asking God for
forgiveness or
alms.

SEE IF THEY WET THEIR PANTS

The words Guru, Swami, Super Swami, Master, Teacher, Murshid,
Yogi, Priest,

most of those sporting such a title are
just peacocks.

The litmus test is:
hold them upside down over a cliff for a few hours.
If they don't wet their
pants

maybe you found a real
one.

SEASONS IN THE MIND

There are seasons in the mind,
great currents and winds move there,

the true yogi ties a rein to them; a power plant
he becomes.

Winter, spring, summer, fall: these are pages
in a book the advanced can turn to,
and impart.

Order is a great benefit to the seeker,
otherwise living in one's own house can become as
walking through a marketplace

where all the merchants keep shouting,
"You owe me."

That does not sound like
much fun,

and who could accomplish anything
in all that
noise.

THE SLIGHTEST IDEA

The moon
and I call each other moon.
And the sun and I call each other sun,
all while this truth also
exists:

I have been so crazy in love with the earth for the last fifty years
that not for one second have I lifted
my head out from beneath
her skirt.

Who
is that
wild looking character then,
who can shop in the market and tend for his family,
that some may call
Kabir?

I don't have the
slightest
idea.

VISITING HOLY SHRINES

If you circumambulated every holy shrine in the world
ten times,

it would not get you to heaven
as quick

as controlling your
anger.

AN INTELLIGENT RICH PERSON

I don't think there is such a thing as
an intelligent mega-rich
person.

For who with a fine mind can look
out upon this world and
hoard

what can nourish
a thousand
souls.

PROFESSIONAL COUNSELING

From the Ocean I heard a million fish say,
"Give me a beer—quick."

I replied, "Dears, how can that be? How can a fish in the water
want a drink?"

Well, that's how wacky things have gotten. Who else
but Maya could pull a fast one like that
and get away
with
it?

Seriously speaking though:

The fish in the water that is thirsty needs
serious professional

c
o
u
n
s
e
l
i
n
g
.

HIT THE FAN

When God says to God, "Where are you?"

Watch out—duck, for the shit

is going to hit

the

f

a

n

.

I WOULD BE GLAD

You are sitting in a wagon being
drawn by a horse whose
reins you
hold.

There are two inside of you
who can steer.

Though most never hand the reins to Me
so they go from place to place the
best they can, though
rarely happy.

And rarely does their whole body laugh
feeling God's poke
in the
ribs.

If you feel tired, dear,
my shoulder is soft,
I'd be glad to
steer a
while.

SOON WE MAY BE KISSING

There is dew
on these poems in the morning,
and at night a cool breeze may rise from them.

In the winter they are blankets, in the summer a place to swim.

I like talking to you like this. Have you moved
a step closer?

Soon we may be
kissing.

HOW HUMBLE IS GOD?

How humble is God?

God is the tree in the forest that
allows itself to die and will not defend itself in front of those
with the ax, not wanting to cause them
shame.

And God is the earth that will allow itself to
be deformed by man's tools, but He cries; yes, God cries,
but only in front of His closest ones.

And a beautiful animal is being beaten to death,
but nothing can make God break His silence
to the masses
and say,

"Stop, please stop, why are you doing this
to Me?"

How humble is God?
Kabir wept
when I
knew.

A GREAT PILGRIMAGE

I felt in need of a great pilgrimage
so I sat still for three
days

and God came
to me.

WHERE THE SHOPKEEPER WOULD SAY

I was

looking for that shop

where the shopkeeper would say,

"There is nothing of value in here."

I found it and did

not leave.

The richness of not wanting

wrote these

poems.

I HAD TO SEEK THE PHYSICIAN

I had to seek the Physician
because of the pain this world
caused
me.

I could not believe what happened when I got there—
I found my
Teacher.

Before I left, he said,
"Up for a little homework, yet?"
"Okay," I replied.

"Well then, try thanking all the people
who have caused
you pain.

They helped you
come to
me."

MAYBE IT WILL BECOME CHIC

I was invited
to an important conference
where many learned men from different countries
were all going to address the topic:

Where Is God?

I was wearing my best clothes and had even fasted for a week,
hoping to help sharpen my mind. Just before I was to leave though,
I felt powerfully drawn to a little shrine in my bedroom,
and I went there and knelt to pray.

I could not believe what then happened:
Kali threw her arms around me and started tearing at my clothes,
then she started throwing delicious food into my mouth,
purposely missing several times it seemed,
thus soiling my pundit attire;

and then she made me perform many times as if I were her
husband; then she said, "Now Kabir, don't be late for that big talk,
and don't change your clothes—I like that love-stained look;
maybe it will become chic?"

I arrived just as it was my turn to stand before this august crowd,
and apologized for my appearance.

"So Where Is God?" the head of the conference says to me.

"Well, (well, I stammered) if you really want to know the truth—if
you hurry—you might catch Her legs still spread
back at my
pad."

Kali: A (very wild) Hindu Goddess

STAY WITH ME A WHILE

I lived with her night and day—
the Nag.

I don't mean my wife or mother-in-law,
they are both angels.

I am talking about that voice in me that would not
let me hold each moment
as I did my son when
he was born.

How to slay the Nag?

I am afraid I have become fond of you,
dear student,

if I spoke the answer,
you might
run.

SPECULATIVE

I had been asking God for a sign to help me
with a big business
decision.

I was walking by the river and a flock of geese
were coming in for a landing and all
passed right over my head—
and relieved themselves.

I became covered with bird shit
and decided to never
invest in anything

speculative.

KABIR, THE OIL IT BURNS

I am
standing
naked in the marketplace
but no one turns their head to look at me,
for no one can see me
as I am.

Still I offer my friendship to all,
still to each wing and fin and cell—I will be forever in obeisance.
Anyone who bows touches my feet;
anyone who sings helps me in my work.
All labor is because my
sinew quivers.

I cover
the divine flame in my heart,
for if I turned God loose from my house
the earth would reveal to your eyes what mine always see—
existence is a lamp and Kabir,
the oil it
burns.

The king is in a mood to grant pardons to acts yet done.
If you can understand that kind of power, that is dormant in you,
you may be ready for a teacher
like Kabir.

I am standing naked in the world forever in homage
to all movement. I cherish every atom
that He moves in this
dance.

WHERE DO THE EYES OF WOMEN FALL?

If your
pockets were happy with coins and into a fancy
store they brought you

where would the eyes of women
fall?

Our clothes chat with other clothes as they pass,
though who but a sweet young creature could care
so much about how they
look?

But if a mirror ever makes
you sad

you should know
that it does
not know
you.

THE PAST'S LIPS ARE NOT DECEASED

Why not look at the beauty your
memory holds,

so nourishing that light can be.

The past's lips are not
deceased.

Let them comfort you
if they
can.

IT STOPS WORKING

Look
what happens to the scale
when love
holds
it.

It
stops
working.

NO HARM DONE

There is a sword in a museum not far from me.
It was once used by a great prince
who defended his country
and faith,

and many limbs and heads it
severed.

One day that sword will die as all things will,
and it will stand before God

and the sword's eyes will behold the splendor
of heaven behind our Beloved, and the sword will wonder
with all of its heart, "Will He let me in,
because of my
life?"

And God will say to that sword, as He does
to every creature,

"No harm done. No harm done.

Forever welcomed
are all."

Mira

The moon was perched
like a golden hawk on the mango tree.
I knew the moon was like me—in heat, crazed and hunting.
So I climbed up there with that wild old gal thinking:
two drunk beauties like us will surely
snag Krishna with our eyes.

Mirabai (c. 1498–1550) is the most renowned woman poet-saint of India, her songs sung by Hindus, Muslims, and Sikhs alike. She was born a princess in the area of Rajasthan. Her great-grandfather founded the city of Jodhpur.

It has been said that when Mira was a small child she brought a plate of food to a *sadhu* (a wandering ascetic) at the palace gate. He whispered a few words in her ear and bestowed a tiny statue of Krishna into her hand, which she forever treasured. There are no other accounts of her having had a teacher or formal religious instruction, so perhaps those few words held some key to a spiritual awakening. Some time later she questioned her mother about who would be her husband, as marriages were often arranged in the early years of a girl's life. Her mother, perhaps not fathoming the seriousness of her daughter's inquiry, playfully pointed to the little statue of Krishna and answered that he would be Mira's groom. From that time onward Mira felt herself to be married to Krishna, and when the time came for her actual marriage, she refused to submit to being treated as a piece of property within the conventional marriage that had been arranged for her against her will.

Her husband died soon after their marriage, and this allowed Mira to begin leading a more religious life, toward which she had long felt inclined. She began seeking out the company of wandering *sadhus* and felt drawn to public temples that were usually only visited by low-caste devotees. Her presence at these temples, and her singing and dancing and embracing of untouchables enraged her in-laws to such an extreme that they tried to kill her. Mira, when in her early thirties, renounced her title and position and fled. She herself became a *sadhu*, traveling much of northwestern India on foot, sleeping often in the open, sometimes near temples and mosques.

She was a fierce champion of human rights, especially women's rights, and with a shocking wit and penetrating insight would often expose the ridiculous aspects of politics, orthodox religion, the caste system, and chauvinistic oppression. Her songs often glorified the ascetic's life, and at times her poetry was very erotic. As a finely educated woman, she first composed her poems/songs in the ancient tradition of classical Indian poetry. In fact, Mira's love songs are said to have helped revitalize and evolve North Indian music. Even today her songs are very popular and sung by classical singers as well as heard throughout the streets of cities and in villages. Several thousand poems are attributed to her though perhaps only a few hundred are authentic. There is an account of a childhood handmaid of Mira, named Lalita, who may have followed her on her wanderings for a while, noting the songs down in a notebook. Records in the Ranchhorji temple at the coastal city of Dwarka, where Mira is last recorded as having lived, mention such a notebook.

Mira spent the last few years of her life attending the destitute near the Ranchhorji temple and writing poems until she joined her Lord.

SUCH WISDOM

You should act more responsibly, God,
with all that gorgeousness you
possess.

You have made all of my friends nuts
and basically unfit to do much else but dream of you—and
plot drawing your mouth
close again.

The soup kitchens are complaining
about our wisdom of
getting drunk
all day

on the gossip we
share about
you.

I GET DIZZY

I can't forget about love
for more than two
seconds.

I get dizzy if I think about anything
but the way you pant
in my
ear.

IN FRONT OF HIS WIFE

I tried controlling myself but it did no good.
My senses are
aflame.

I heard You singing.
That started all my blessed madness.

I openly made love with everything in sight last night
and this morning

the constable showed up and wrote out twenty citations.

I guess I should not have jumped naked
on him in front
of his
wife.

The hypocrite, he wouldn't have complained
at all

if we were
alone.

A HUNDRED OBJECTS CLOSE BY

I know a cure for sadness:
Let your hands touch something that
makes your eyes
smile.

I bet there are a hundred objects close by
that can do that.

Look at
beauty's gift to us—
her power is so great she enlivens
the earth, the sky, our
soul.

AND HELP HIM COMFORT

God has
a special interest in women
for they can lift this world to their breast
and help Him
comfort.

WHAT SHOULD I TELL THE OTHER GIRLS?

I would not have set foot on this earth
if my Lover had not come.

And what would I care for looking at form
if you God had not sanctified all with your touch.

The promise of your lips
tricked me.

Since I heard your name, I have been so eager
for us to embrace,

why, Lord, did you make me stand
in line?

I got my arms around you last night.
What should I tell the
other girls?

He was worth waiting for—
indeed!

ONE'S MIND

He was too shy to sing,
but I taught
Him.

The Sky's voice is such that
one's mind must be very
quiet to hear
God

speak.

A GREAT YOGI

In my travels I spent time with a great yogi.
Once he said to me,

"Become so still you hear the blood flowing
through your veins."

One night as I sat in quiet,
I seemed on the verge of entering a world inside so vast
I know it is the source of
all of
us.

I WANT YOU TO HAVE THIS

I
want
you to have
this,

all the beauty in my eyes, all the grace of my mouth,
all the splendor of my
strength,

all the
wonder of the musk parts
of my
body,

for are we
not talking about real love, real
love?

I WRITE OF THAT JOURNEY

I remember how my mother would hold me.
I would look up at her sometimes and see her weep.

I understand now what was happening.
Love so strong a force
it broke the
cage,

and she disappeared from everything
for a blessed
moment.

All actions have evolved
from the taste of flight;
the hope of freedom
moves our cells
and limbs.

Unable to live on the earth, Mira ventured out alone in the sky—
I write of that journey
of becoming as
free as
God.

Don't forget love;
it will bring all the madness you need
to unfurl yourself across
the universe.

TWO DRUNK BEAUTIES

The moon was perched like a golden hawk on
the mango tree.

I knew the moon was like me—in heat,
crazed and hunting.

So I climbed up there with that wild old gal—
thinking:

Two drunk beauties like us
will surely snag
Krishna

with our
eyes.

USE THE GEOMETRY

He left His fingerprint on a glass the
earth drinks
from.

Every religion has studied it.
Churches and temples use the geometry of those lines
to establish rites and laws and prayers
and our ideas of the
universe.

I guess there is just no telling how out of hand—and wonderfully wild—
things will get

when our lips catch up to

His.

IS ALL THIS GOD STUFF REAL?

Girls, think twice before inviting God near.
His charms will turn you into a slave—are you ready for such
a wonderful bondage?

What if your human lover is just about ready to insert
a pulsating mass into your forest
and rain there;

what if just as he/she enters
—you hear His flute
calling,

could you run outside in a second, naked, and ready for
the world to make fun of you;

for who can really see Him.
Everyone may think you are worshiping a mirage.

And what if He asked you to give all your gold bangles
and fine cloths to the next
beggar you see?

Giving him our clay (our body) to shape is one thing,
for this can excite us,

but when our jewelry and silk are at risk
surely it is time to seriously ask

is all this God stuff—
real?

THE EARTH—MY OWN BODY I EXPLORED

One night as I walked in the desert
the mountains rode on my
shoulders

and the sky became my heart,
and the earth—my own body, I explored.

Every object began to wink at me, and Mira wisely
calculated the situation, thinking:
My charms must be at
their height—

now would be a good time to
rush into His
arms,

maybe He won't drop me
so quick.

REDEEM THAT GENDER

Living with that guy, how could you have not gone nuts;
I bet he even lied, the
coward.

I know why God comes to this earth as man,
in hopes of redeeming
that gender.

God knows he owes us women—
big time,

for the way those brutes
usually
act.

KEEP DOING THAT

Love, you have wrecked my body.
Keep doing
that.

I am more well with this deep ache
of missing
you

than content with the
physical wonders
you can pacify
us with.

OUR EYES SHOULD BE

The
rejected lover trembles
like when the earth quakes.

An oasis for each other our eyes should be.

All hearts listen: I rarely get angry
but if you hold another close
and then cast them
aside

you will have Mira
to deal
with.

A LIMB JUST MOVED

You taught Your songs to the birds first,
why was that?

And You practiced Your love in the hearts of animals
before You created man.

I know the planets talk at night
and tell secrets
about
You.

A limb just moved before me,
the beauty of this world
is causing me to
weep.

PREFERENCE

Stuck with another day,
how should we
pass
it?

If anything worked for you before
—I'd give that

preference.

EVEN LONGER FOR HER

Three years went by and I had not
slept with a
man.

I consulted the moon about this
and she said,

it had even been longer
for her,

but she didn't think she was
missing much.

FRAGILE

So fragile this petal the earth,

as fragile as

love.

THE WAY THEY HELD EACH OTHER

A woman and her young daughter were destitute
and traveling to another country
where they hoped to find
a new life.

Three men stole them while they were camping.

They were brought to a city
and sold as slaves; each to a different
owner.

They were given one minute more together,
before their fates became unknown.

My soul clings to God like that,
the way they held
each other.

A SCHOLAR, A LAWYER, AND A PRIEST

In my travels, I came upon a village that had
a new temple built over a big well, but no one could draw
water from it without paying a price.

I asked about this, and this story was told:

One hundred years ago, there was a group of boys that
would go to the well to swim, that is, all but one would
dive from the top, for one was crippled and could only watch.
With all his heart he would wish he was like
his friends, that his one arm and leg had not been limp
since he was born.

One day, when it was especially hot, and he was watching
his friends cut up and laugh at the bottom of the well,
they all turned to him and stared in awe as if
seeing something miraculous.

The crippled boy turned around and Krishna
was standing there smiling wonderfully, and said,

"It sure is hot today, climb on my back—
we will dive in." And they did.

Krishna never came up from the bottom of the well,
it is said, and when the child who
had been on the back of Krishna came up,
he was no longer crippled and remained healed the rest of his life.

The fame of the well spread and many legends and rumors naturally
evolved and began to circulate.
But the water remained free, and hundreds would
travel to drink it and camp there at night
and tell the different stories they had heard; the point being,
they would be thinking of the Lord and participating in the stories,
in a way that helped them most.

If one unveiled word from God touched this earth it would
ignite like a rag soaked in oil.
All we can bear of the Truth is hearsay and rumors.
In this starving world what feeds—let feed!
Best that many dishes are set before us and as we become less caged
we will pick wisely like the golden falcon over fertile plains,
like the mountain deer in spring lush valleys.

A scholar, a lawyer, and a priest arrived one day
and all pissed in the water, so to speak.

What the priest and the scholar wanted the people to believe
got printed in books, which they also sold along with the water,
and of course the lawyer made their insanity legal.

The water I tasted was sour.
I think Krishna left.

In this sorrowful world why tamper
with anything that lifts
our spirits.

I'D CALL THAT

Before I
fell asleep last night
I laid awake and wondered:

What did I achieve this day
just roaming around calling His name?

So I brought before my mind's eye all who I had been kind to,
and it turned out to be
all things that
I had
seen.

I'd call that—one hell of a
productive
day!

MIRA KNOWS WHY

The earth looked at Him and began to dance.
Mira knows why, for her soul too
is in love.

If you cannot picture God
in a way that always
strengthens
you,

you need to read
more of my
poems.

St. Teresa of Avila

*I found completeness when each breath
began to silently say the name of my Lord.*

Teresa of Avila (1515–1582) is undoubtedly the most influential female saint in the Western world, and she has made great contributions to spiritual literature and poetry. She was a woman of tremendous courage who is rightfully credited with remarkable political and religious reform achieved against the strongest—and most insidious—chauvinistic forces.

A realistic picture of Teresa's life did not even reach the English-reading general public until the 1960s. She was known to have had a remarkable quick wit and a stunning, even provocative, sense of humor, as well as great physical beauty. Her complete works include seven books, four hundred and fifty letters, and assorted poetry. Her writings are considered masterpieces of mystical prose and verse. She personally founded seventeen Carmelite convents and two monasteries, despite enormous opposition from the Church and other men in power.

Teresa was born in Avila, a beautiful high mountain village of the Sierra de Gredos. She was one of thirteen children, three girls and ten boys, in a wealthy family. The Spain in which Teresa grew up was permeated with seven hundred years of Arabian culture; the eradication of Arab power was followed by one of Spain's darkest periods, the insanity of the Inquisitions, which, in the fourteenth century, along with other grievous deeds, forced mass conversions of Jews to Christianity. *Conversos*, as they were called, were a continually persecuted minority with special taxes, exclusion from Church or military professions, and even service in the New World (at this time most young males sought to make their fortune in the New World as did nine of Teresa's ten brothers). Teresa's grandfather, a wealthy wool and silk merchant, had actually reclaimed his Jewish ancestry, partly for business reasons (the aristocracy protected and even intermarried with Jews) although the family had been *conversos* for over one hundred years. However, before the end of the fourteenth century, the anti-Semetic atmosphere in Toledo, where the family then lived, became so extreme that Teresa's father, Alonso Sanchez, moved the family to Avila and aspired to live the life of the *hidalgo* class, giving up his father's cloth trade and living off his savings. Inflation was rampant because of the great quantities of gold and silver brought in from the New World, and by the time Alonso Sanchez died, his family was bankrupt.

Teresa was her father's favorite child, and the most spirited. Her mother died during childbirth when Teresa was thirteen, after which she had little supervision. It is believed she had a lover at the age of fifteen, which caused her father to send her to a convent boarding school, only to see her return home two years later because of poor health. When she was twenty-one, Teresa ran away from home to join a convent. At that time many convents were more like hotels for women, allowing them a great deal more independence than they would be allowed at home, though after two years at the convent Teresa had a near-death experience that changed her life. A spiritual awakening began in which she cultivated a system of meditation that sought quieting the mind to such an extent that God could then be heard speaking. Over the next twenty years she experienced many mystical states but not until she was fifty did she begin the most far-reaching aspects of her life's work.

Teresa had a great desire for learning and when the Inquisition, in 1559, forbade women to read, Teresa turned to God and asked Him to teach her soul about divine love. She then began to write completely out of her own experience. Many of her poems are, in fact, intimate accounts of her communion with God.

The Church's persecution of Teresa had not waned when she passed away and was buried in Alba de Tormes in 1582. A year after her death some of her disciples, feeling that she might have wished to be buried in Avila, had her body exhumed. When her body was found to be perfectly intact and emitting a wonderful fragrance, her sainthood was formally decreed, allowing the publication and preservation of some of her works.

Most of what we see today of Teresa's work is probably reined way back, for her writings fell into the hands and under the control of the very forces that had so opposed her throughout her life. With this in mind the versions that follow attempt to portray a—hopefully—more genuine account of her astounding relationship with God.

I WILL JUST SAY THIS

We
bloomed in Spring.

Our bodies
are the leaves of God.

The apparent seasons of life and death
our eyes can suffer;

but our souls, dear, I will just say this forthright:
they are God
Himself,

we will never perish
unless He
does.

EVERY PROPHET'S NAME

I found completeness
when each breath began to silently say the name
of my Lord.

That name—my conception of Him—extended to me
a hand that led to a place
where even His divine name could not exist.
Why?

Most sounds express discontent, longing, or negotiation.
The teapot may whistle out an ecstatic cry,
but even that I learned to control
until everything I knew burst
in a glorious symmetry.

I have no seams, no walls, no laws.
My frontiers and God's are the same.

One Divine Being is existence.
All the forests on this earth combined are but
a tiny wood fiber—a particle of one spoke
on the Wheel.

What is the relationship of form to the unseen aspects of God?

What percentage of God is unseen?
What percentage of the Truth of Him do we know?

He led me to a place where only Light existed.
Only in us is God so lost that He asks
questions.

The soul outside all walls
never troubles Him, never wonders things like,
"Where are You,
Beloved?"

For then your arms and God's
are intertwined.

I said to my Lord,
"This Holy place I have entered—
is Your name the only key
to this?"

And my Lord responded,
"How old do you think is existence?
For eons of time, souls have been entering Me;

every Prophet's name is a key,
as is every heart full of
forgiveness
and love."

HE DESIRED ME SO I CAME CLOSE

He desired me so I came close.

No one can near God unless He has
prepared a bed for
you.

A thousand souls hear His call every second,
but most every one then looks into their life's mirror and
says, "I am not worthy to leave this
sadness."

When I first heard His courting song, I too
looked at all I had done in my life
and said,

"How can I gaze into His omnipresent eyes?"
I spoke those words with all
my heart,

but then He sang again, a song even sweeter,
and when I tried to shame myself once more from His presence
God showed me His compassion and spoke a divine truth,

"I made you, dear, and all I make is perfect.
Please come close, for I
desire
you."

IF THE SUN TOOK YOU IN HIS ARMS

When my mouth touched His I became invisible,
the way the earth would if the sun
took it into
its arms.

The ecstatic death I know. What can touch His exquisite form
is not anything that can
be seen.

How do we make love to God;
how does the soul make love
to God?

How does the soul
make love to
God?

The heart has divine instincts;
it just needs to be turned loose in the sky.

Does not every angel know where
He lives,

and will beat on His door all night
if it is locked.

LAUGHTER CAME FROM EVERY BRICK

Just these two words He spoke
changed my life,

"Enjoy Me."

What a burden I thought I was to carry—
a crucifix, as did He.

Love once said to me, "I know a song,
would you like to hear it?"

And laughter came from every brick in the street
and from every pore
in the sky.

After a night of prayer, He
changed my life when
He sang,

"Enjoy Me."

NOT YET TICKLED

How did those priests ever get so serious
and preach all that
gloom?

I don't think God
tickled them
yet.

Beloved—hurry.

YOUR PLAYMATES

I was born for you;
what do you want of me, dear?

Look at all that has come from your wish:
the forests, the streams, the mountains,
the fields, every creature:
are these not your
playmates?

Do we give you comfort, God,
in Eternity?

We were born for you; don't be shy, Beloved.
Just tell us what you want

but in a language
that makes us
smile.

CLARITY IS FREEDOM

I had tea yesterday with a great theologian,
and he asked me,

"What is your experience of God's will?"

I liked that question—
for the distillation of thought hones thought in others.
Clarity, I know, is freedom.

What is my experience of God's will?

Everyone is a traveler. Most all need lodging, food,
and clothes.

I let enter my mouth what will enrich me. I wear what
will make my eye content,
I sleep where I will
wake with the
strength to
deeply
love

all my mind can
hold.

What is God's will for a wing?
Every bird knows
that.

KNOW, DEAR, KNOW

I thought of putting my hand where I could tell no one,
on that part of my soul that is always warm.
I knew a sacred liquid there could
flow and give me
peace.

And my soul, I have come to see
is both spirit and
flesh.

The body is a nest I do not mourn when I fly, do you?

Why should I not give to myself
what a tender skilled husband could and remain free
of the external bindings of
another?

And God replied, "To those who are married
to me, I'll take care of things like that."

But what if you get busy with your other wives
and forget about my loneliness?

And again He spoke, saying, "I have not forgotten the thought of
any creature that ever lived.

If I do not take you into my arms as you might want,

know, dear, know, it is for
the upliftment of all.

And if I do come to you in a dream
and satisfy the most intimate of your physical desires,
know, dear, know, it is for
the upliftment
of all.

And all I am constantly
drawing
close."

CONCEPTS, A JAR WE BREAK

Anxious to see you, I died to the world.

Hearing your voice at the city's edge,
at the horizon of form and space,

how could I then notice anything hands made;
how could I adore or suffer
time?

Anxious to hold you, I forgot myself completely
but you did not care about the way I came to look; I mean
your shape and mine, what were those?—

the seed husk that falls,

because it could not contain our mingled feet.

Anxious to see you, our souls became your glory,
our eyes became your fire.

All concepts of God are like a jar
we break,

because only the infinite can
contain our perfect
love.

AS I FOUND THE SOURCE

When your soul was born,
it was like a still ocean that had yet to experience
its infinite life.

God then came to the shores of our souls and gazed upon the
immaculate splendor that His divine heart created.

He then took off His clothes and dove into us.

Nothing on their own have your arms ever done,
the movements of your feet are caused
by the waves He stirred.

Light baptizes life wherever it falls,
and every religion and all upon this earth
is a shadow.

A shadow may move but it has no real power of its own,
though it can affect the weak and frighten them, and men can use
that darkness to exploit others.

As I found the source of all we do, as I found the
source of all our desires, so humble God became
He admitted: "Yes, I caused
all things."

IN A WAY THE GRAIN CAN FEEL

Remember, God, that we are the plants in your fields
so connected to the
earth

that you know what would happen
if you did not rain
upon us.

And if your light ceased to lift us from the ground
and craft our bodies,

how might we near you like the
suns?

Remember, God, to love us in a way
our souls can taste
and rejoice
in.

FEELING DESPERATE

The
earth
and sky will open their purse for you
and your life will
change

if with all your heart you say these words each day,
"Teach me, dear God, all that you
know."

One night I walked through the streets feeling
desperate, in need of
alchemy.

A hooded priest passed by where there were no lamps.
I could not see his face, I only heard these words that he
kept repeating,

"Teach me, dear Lord, all that you know."

I knew a treasure had
entered my
soul.

THE SERVANT OF UNITY

Most men in power have not the strength or wisdom
to be satisfied with the way
things are.

The sane know contentment, for beauty is their lover,
and beauty is never absent from this world.

The farther away light is from one's touch
the more one naturally speaks of the
need for change.

Yes, overthrow any government inside
that makes you weep.

The child blames the external and focuses his energies there;
the warrior conquers the realms within
and becomes
gifted.

Only the inspired should make decisions
that affect the lives of many,

never a man who has not held God in his arms
and become the servant of
unity.

THE GRAIL

They are like shy, young school kids—time and space,
before the woman and the man who are
intimate with God.

The realized soul can play with this universe
the way a child can a ball.

A chalice—the Grail—my body became, for it held the Christ
and He drank
from me.

Sanctified are our limbs,
for every heart has touched God, though most with closed eyes.

A holy relic is each creature, and beauty may worry
about its comeliness waning.

We fear dying till we know the truth of ourselves.

The seams on my body
are torn;

I have stepped from that region of me
that did not love
all the
time.

There is a divine world of light
with many suns in
the sky.

I slept with my Lord
one night,

now all that is luminous
I know we

conceived.

MORE TRAFFIC THAN YOU THINK

God stood at the shore of Himself and dove in.
How can He do things like that?
Anything *goes* with
the Big Guy, I
guess.

A divine splash happened,
billions of drops were propelled into space.

I said to a drop shooting past me one night,
"Where ya going, what's the hurry,
slow down."

It did, and we talked for a while, that drop and I;
some angels too
came by.

There is more traffic than you think—
cruising.

WHEN THE HOLY THAWS

A woman's body, like the earth, has seasons;
when the mountain stream flows,
when the holy
thaws,

when I am most fragile and in need,
it was then, it seems,
God came
closest.

God, like a medic on a field, is tending our souls.
Our horns get locked with desires, but don't hold yourself
too accountable; for all desires are
really innocent. That is what
the compassion in His
eyes tells me.

Why this great war between the countries—the countries—
inside of us?

What are all these insane borders we protect?
What are all these different names for the same church of love
we kneel in together? For it is true, together we live; and only
at that shrine where all are welcome will God sing
loud enough to be heard.

Our horns got locked with the earth and sky in some odd
marriage ritual; so what, don't worry. We should be proud of
ourselves for everything we helped create in this
magic world.

And God is always there, if you feel wounded. He kneels
over this earth like
a divine medic,

and His love thaws
the holy in
us.

I LOVED WHAT I COULD LOVE

I had a natural passion for fine clothes, excellent food, and
lively conversation about all matters that concern
the heart still alive. And even a passion
about my own
looks.

Vanities: they do not exist.

Have you ever walked across a stream stepping on
rocks so not to spoil a pair of shoes?

All we can touch, swallow, or say
aids in our crossing to God
and helps unveil the
soul.

Life smooths us, rounds, perfects, as does the river the stone,
and there is no place our Beloved is not flowing
though the current's force you
may not always
like.

Our passions help to lift us.

I loved what I could love until I held Him,
for then—all things—every world
disappeared.

TOO IN LOVE TO CHAT

His hands can shape through ours.
And our sounds can somehow echo what God has never
said,

for the Divine is really speechless, it is
too in love to
chat.

The Holy Wind ruffled our hair and caused
a lot of commotion:

We think God made some rules
but how can that be true when our souls
are really the
governor
of all.

His mind can shape through ours.
Our bodies—and the earth—are as clay. Is
that not so, my
dear.

I have a lovely habit:
at night in my prayers I touch everyone
I have seen that
day;

I shape my heart like theirs
and theirs like
mine.

THE SKY'S SHEETS

When He touches me I clutch the sky's sheets,
the way other
lovers
do

the earth's weave
of clay.

Any real ecstasy is a sign
you are moving
in the right
direction,

don't let any prude tell
you otherwise.

CRAZY

From a distance all want to enter His house.

Once near, watch out for the guard dogs—

both four-legged and two.

Some of them are

crazy as

hell.

DESIRE IN HER SOUL

I wanted
to hold Him as an infant,
what woman would not find that desire
in her soul?

Yes, I wanted to hold Him when He was so in need,
that He might cling to me with
all His strength for
protection.

I never thought of the sun as being maternal
but is there anything that does not
nurse light?

One day I was carrying my wash, one day I was carrying bread,
one day I was carrying a small goat,

and all of them became
my Lord.

I collapsed
on the ground the first time this happened,
the first time the universe
suckled
me.

I WOULD CEASE TO BE

God

dissolved

my mind—my separation.

I cannot describe now my intimacy with Him.

How dependent is your body's life on water and food and air?

I said to God, "I will always be unless you cease to Be,"

and my Beloved replied, "And I

would cease to Be

if you

died."

St. John of the Cross

My soul is a candle that burned away the veil;
only the glorious duties of light I now have.

St. John of the Cross (1542–1591) has long been recognized as one of the world's great mystical poets. His verse reveals a profound, tender experience of divine communion.

St. John was born Juan de Yepes y Alvarez in Fontiveros, Spain, a town northeast of Avila. Like St. Teresa, his family had been Jewish and were *conversos*—"forced Christians." His father was from a wealthy silk merchant family that disowned him when he married a poor orphaned girl (possibly of Moorish descent) from Toledo. St. John's father died when John was quite young, leaving a widow and three sons in deep poverty. His mother loomed, and John became a carpenter, painter, and tailor to help support the family. While in his teens they moved to Medina del Campo, a larger and more prosperous city, where he worked for a while at a hospital. It was during this period that he received his first formal education at a Jesuit school. He was an exceptional student, learned Latin well, and stayed in this school until the age of twenty-one. Then, without much consultation with anyone, he became a Carmelite friar and subsequently spent four years at the University of Salamanca.

When St. John was twenty-five years old, a decisive event occurred in his life. He met St. Teresa and was remarkably affected, one could say transformed, by her. She was in her fifties and emanated great spiritual power and insight. It is believed that they fell in love (in the purest sense) with each other. It is reported that she once remarked of St. John, "He was the most angelic human being I have ever encountered." In 1568, John agreed to start the first reformed monastery for Carmelite friars in a dilapidated farmhouse that Teresa had received from a benefactor. In 1572, he became the confessor for the nuns at the convent of the Incarnation in Avila where St. Teresa had been appointed prioress.

In 1577, as a result of the attempted reform of the Carmelite order and his alliance with St. Teresa, he was kidnapped and imprisoned at Toledo. It was during this period of debased confinement and torture by his fellow priests that he miraculously composed some of his greatest poetry.

For much of the nine months St. John was in prison, he was confined to a tiny cell, actually an unlit closet in which he could not even stand up. He was left to relieve himself on the floor of this tiny cell, and his few scraps of food and water were sometimes thrown into his feces and urine. On a regular basis he was brought from his cell and beaten by some of the other *priests*, to the extent that he became permanently crippled. He was not given a change of clothes or allowed to wash for months. He became infested with lice and developed acute dysentery. He was forced to sleep upon his own excrement. This prison was in the basement of a *monastery*. One night in prayer, asking God for the strength to endure his confinement and torture, St. John had this remarkable experience or vision. He heard a duet in which God and he were the singers:

"I am dying of love darling, what should I do?"

And the Beloved responded,

"Then die my sweetheart—just die. Die to all that is not us; what could be more beautiful."

The Prophet Muhammad once said, "Die before you die," and a contemporary religious figure, Meher Baba, once said, "Being is dying by loving." Both are speaking of an important transformative juncture through which we will all pass. "My soul is a candle that burned away the veil," says St. John, the veil being that which separates us from God. The veil being the false, the untruths we believe, that we must someday die to, before we are *born*.

Following this vision life changed remarkably for St. John for a while. He was given better care and even pen and paper by a new jailer, and during the next few weeks wrote down some thirty stanzas of "Cantico Espiritual" and completed "La fonte" and probably "Noche Oscura" (Black Night), which is really a love poem about transformation.

On the eve of the Assumption of the Virgin the head of the monastery pulled St. John from his tiny cell and hideously beat him, promising that he would be released if he would just abandon the Reform movement. That night the Virgin appeared to St. John, filling his cell and heart with a divine comfort, and saying, "My darling, I have accepted your surrender to all that has happened here as you believed it was God's will, but now I command you to escape." And within a few days he miraculously did escape.

The most prolific period of his life followed his imprisonment. In solitude, surrounded by the clarity and beauty of the Andalusian landscape he came to know days of heaven on earth.

On December 14, 1591, just before midnight, St. John, lying near death and remarkably weak, wanted to fix his bed as if someone important were coming to visit. He then asked that the "Song of Songs" be read. And while he was listening, suddenly he exclaimed: "So beautiful are the flowers!" and died.

BELOVED

God held
the earth as if it were His lover
and spoke with the most tender of feelings
to all in existence as He spoke
to me,

"Look, dear son, I have made a bride for you,
but she is shy; so how are you
to consummate?

I want all souls to consummate with me,
so I devised a plan:

As each soul nears heaven differences will dissolve to such
a sublime extent that when the heart looks upon
any object in this world it
will cry 'Beloved'

and passionately run into
an embrace with
me."

That blessed grace I now know.
I now see my Beloved
everywhere.

WHY DOES NOT THE CHURCH TELL YOU?

At last the time came for the bride
to be with Him.

Nothing all the other brides had ever known
could have prepared me.

Only the beauty and light you cannot describe
has a place in His house.

I can touch God—yes—but not with anything I own,
not with anything I can identify with,
not with anything that
knows
me.

Purity, have you ever contemplated that word?
I once beheld the root of the Immaculate
and it drew me into itself,

I looked at all through
His eyes.

Why does not my sacred church tell you:
God only sees
Himself.

I AM WHAT IS LOVED

I said to God,

"What are you?" And He replied,

"I am what is loved. I am not what should be loved

for how cruel that would then

be for my

bride."

MY SOUL IS A CANDLE

My soul is a candle that burned away the veil;
only the glorious duties of light I now have.

The sufferings I knew initiated me into God.
I am a holy confessor for men.

When I see their tears running across their cheeks
and falling into
His hands,

what can I say to their great sorrow
that I too have
known.

The soul is a candle that will burn away the darkness,
only the glorious duties of love we will have.

The sufferings I knew initiated me into God.
Only His glorious cares
I now have.

IF YOU WANT

If
you want,
the Virgin will come walking down the road
pregnant with the holy,
and say,

"I need shelter for the night, please take me inside your heart,
my time is so close."

Then, under the roof of your soul, you will witness the sublime
intimacy, the divine, the Christ
taking birth
forever,

as she grasps your hand for help, for each of us
is the midwife of God, each of us.

Yes there, under the dome of your being does creation
come into existence eternally, through your womb, dear pilgrim—
the sacred womb in your soul,

as God grasps our arms for help; for each of us is
His beloved servant
never
far.

If you want, the Virgin will come walking
down the street pregnant
with Light and
sing . . .

THIS EARTH A BOW

You let
my sufferings cease,
for there was no one who could cure them.

Now let my eyes behold your face for you are our only love.

My spirit's body is rising near—this earth a bow
that shot me;

now lift me into your arms as something precious
that you dropped.

My only suffering, from this day forth,
will be your divine
beauty,

and you will constantly cure my blessed sight each time
you bring your face so near to mine
and call me
bride.

Do not be sad, my old friends; look,
these wings are finally stretched and laughing.

Our souls are rising near to you—this earth a bow that shot us;

now lift me into your arms, dear God,
like something precious that
you dropped.

IS THAT MY FATE?

Do they prove anything to you, these tears?

All that I had I laid outside that door
where I was told you lived, and someone took those gifts,
was it you?

Were they that worthless that no thanks was given?
That must have been the case for I heard
not one word of gratitude.

Has it ever happened that a lover courting a lover
has not offered trinkets? Surely you did
not begrudge me for that.

In the world of amorous play amongst your forest creatures
I have tried to learn some secret about love
to bring you as near as they did; for I see how happy
you made them.

The flame called the moth but the glass pane was there.
How many have died not in the fire but in the cold,
crazed in longing.

Is the fate of any heart to not reach you?

No, no, that is not the fate
of any soul.

WORDS THAT COMFORT GOD

I won't go to sleep tonight until you have spoken to me
those words that you read to yourself
when you need
comfort,
God.

This ceiling post in my room, I will tie my hands to it.
If I sleep it will be standing passed out
in exhaustion from vigil
and prayer.

I don't know, you tell me, Beloved,
how to win your
body,

for I have tried everything, but I
feel so helpless.

I will not lie in my bed again until you have kissed me
with those words that you whisper to yourself,
my Lord, when you need comfort,

when you need
comfort.

THE SLEEPING MAN IS BLESSED

What would a man buried alive do?

Try with all his strength to breathe the sun again, of course.

Your hands, your feet, your eyes,
your every word and
thought,

there is
not one waking
second

the soul pounding against the cage of the body
does not want God

to rush into its
lungs.

The sleeping man is blessed with
a faith that is not
active.

Faith as it ripens turns into an almost insatiable appetite,

and the awake lion must prowl for God
in places it once
feared.

THEY HAVE DIFFERENT NEEDS

Some seeds beneath the earth
are dormant.

They fell the last time the cool air
turned the leaves
gold.

Those seeds have different needs than we do;
let them go about their life
completely unharmed
by your views.

We have cracked open, we sensed
even beneath the earth—
the holy was near,

and are reaching up to know
and claim
light

as our
self.

A NURSERY RHYME

Would not the sun have lost its mind if it said to the moon,
"Dear, give me more light."

For does not all the moon's beauty and charm come from the sun's
existence; could we even see the moon if it was not
for the sun's being?

Is anything we see of earth and sky and each other not dependent
on the Sun, on the real Sun—God? Are we not some extension of His
Being? Does not all form have its life in reflecting Him? It does.

Would not a father have lost his mind if he locked his child
into a room that the child could not possibly escape from, and then
the man beat the child for not being able to escape.

It would be insane of God to ever make
us moons—our souls—feel bad for not giving Him
more light, more love, more obedience,
more anything He might want.

And don't tell me of free will.
That is just a compassionate nursery rhyme

that can be helpful to believe,
if you are

infirm.

THE ESSENCE OF DESIRE

I did not
have to ask my heart what it wanted,
because of all the desires I have ever known just one did I cling to
for it was the essence of
all desire:

to hold beauty in
my soul's
arms.

A VITAL TRUTH

I look
at your body, dear;
I am talking about a woman's,
and I question my vows deeply. For all around me
are making
love.

Beauty is exciting the tree's limbs; look how sweet
they act and sway, they pretend to be shy, then laugh and yield,
as I want to with
you.

Most yield to love when its power awakes.
My hands could kneel upon you. An altar I see your breasts.

And is not every part of me sacred too, worthy of His mouth,
worthy of the earth's homage, worthy of giving
communion.

An altar is every pore and hair on every body—
confess that, dear God,
confess;

why make us suffer your silence any longer
about such a vital
truth?

Still, I shall maintain for reasons beyond all morals,
my blessed vow of
chastity.

IF YOU LOVE

You might quiet the whole world for a second
if you pray.

And if you love, if you
really love,

our guns will
wilt.

I COBBLED THEIR BOOTS

How could I love my fellow men who tortured me?

One night I was dragged into a room
and beaten near death with
their shoes

striking me hundreds of times
in the face, scarring me
forever.

I cried out for God to help, until I fainted.

That night in a dream, in a dream more real than this world,
a strap from the Christ's sandal
fell from my bleeding
mouth,

and I looked at Him and He
was weeping, and
spoke,

"I cobbled their boots;
how sorry
I am.

What moves all things
is God."

IT IS GOD WHO SHOULD ASK

With all humility
I say,

it is God who should ask for forgiveness,
not we, Him.

Someday you will know this.
A saint could
explain.

ARROGANCE

The weight of arrogance is such
that no bird can fly
carrying it.

And the man who feels superior
to others, that man
cannot dance,

the real dance when the soul takes God
into its arms and you both fall
onto your knees in
gratitude,

a blessed gratitude
for life.

WHAT IS GRACE?

"What is grace?" I asked God.

And He said,

"All that happens."

Then He added, when I looked perplexed,

"Could not lovers
say that every moment in their Beloved's arms
was grace?

Existence is my arms,
though I well understand how one can turn
away from
me

until the heart has
wisdom."

DEVELOPMENT

Once I said to God, "How do you teach us?"

And He replied,

"If
you were
playing chess with someone who
had infinite power and infinite knowledge
and wanted to make you a
master of the
game,

where would all the chess
pieces be at every
moment?

Indeed, not only where he wanted them,
but where all were best for your
development;

and that is every situation
of one's
life."

A RABBIT NOTICED MY CONDITION

I was sad one day and went for a walk;
I sat in a field.

A rabbit noticed my condition and
came near.

It often does not take more than that to help at times—

to just be close to creatures who
are so full of knowing,
so full of love
that they don't
—chat,

they just gaze with
their
marvelous understanding.

THEY CAN BE LIKE A SUN

They can be like a sun, words.

They can do for the heart
what light can
for a field.

TENDERLY

Tenderly, I now touch all
things,

knowing one day we will
part.

"DIG HERE," THE ANGEL SAID

She caught me off guard when my soul said to me,
"Have we met?"

So surprised I was to hear her speak like that
I chuckled.

She began to sing a tale: "There was once a hardworking man
who used to worry so much because he could
not feed and clothe his children and
wife the way he wanted.

There was a beautiful little chapel in the village
where the man lived and one day while
he was praying, an angel
appeared.

The angel said, 'Follow me.' And he did out into an ancient forest.
'Now dig here,' the angel said. And the man felt strength in
his limbs he had not known since youth and with just
his bare hands he dug deep and found a
lost treasure, and his relationship
with the world changed."

Finding our soul's beauty does that—gives us
tremendous freedom
from worry.

"Dig here," the angel said—
"in your soul,
in your
soul."

TO THOSE SONGS

Your body is a divine stream,
as is your spirit.

When your two great rivers merge, one voice is found
and the earth applauds
in excitement.

Shrines are erected to those songs
the hand and heart have sung
as they served
the world

with a love, a love
we cherish.

PEACE

Quiet yourself.
Reach out with your mind's skillful hand.
Let it go inside of me
and touch
God.

Don't
be shy, dear.
Every aspect of Light we are meant
to know.

The calm hand holds more
than baskets of goods
from the market.

The calm soul knows more
than anything this world
can offer from her
beautiful
womb.

Tukaram

We are too shrewd to trade something for nothing.
Death to the ego—trading down—are you a madman?
No one kicks a good lover out of bed unless they know they got
two more on the way over.

Tukaram (c.1608–1649) is the most influential figure in the development of Marathi literature, and probably the most famous saint who wrote in that language. He was born in the small village of Dehu on the banks of the river Indrayani in Maharashtra, India, not far from the still-thriving city of Poona. He was remarkably prolific; some attribute 8,000 short poems to him. He wrote entirely in Marathi, an Indian dialect still commonly heard in West Central India. His poems were playful and earthy, sometimes very innocent and sometimes thought-provoking, often changing from serious to comical within a few lines. His poems in the vernacular are called *abhangs*, which are poetic songs of a teaching and devotional nature. Even today many children in India grow up hearing these poems (the milder ones) recited and set to contemporary music. It is commonly believed that Tukaram attained the same spiritual heights as Rumi, Hafiz, and Kabir. Like Hafiz, it is said his poems are an intimate journal of discovering God within. They are also similar to Hafiz's work in their brilliant humor.

Tukaram had no schooling except from his father, who came from the Sudra caste, commonly thought a low caste; at that time the Brahmins would refer to all non-Brahmins as "Sudras." His family owned a little land and made their living by selling their produce. Family legend had it that Tukaram's birth was foretold when Krishna appeared in a dream of a grandparent and directly spoke of how Tukaram would benefit humanity through the great charm of his songs. When he was thirteen years old both his parents passed away and he was forced to support his family. He married young, and his first wife and their children died in a great famine, which changed his views of the world tremendously. He began to deeply question the purpose of life and started spending long periods in solitude. He seems to have had many significant dreams during this period of his life, including one where Krishna supposedly initiated him for some divine work. Another recorded dream is that Krishna brought the great thirteenth-century poet Namdeo to visit Tukaram and informed him that it was his destiny to complete the great poetic outpouring of singing God's praises which Namdeo had begun. It was these poems or *abhangs* (which Tukaram composed) that caused the Brahmin priests and scholars to so persecute him, believing themselves to be the only ones worthy to address and or interpret the great religious books.

During Tukaram's awakening process he was often drawn to some caves in the ancient hills near his village. His favorite retreat was called Bhandara, which contained some relics of Buddhist times. He became increasingly indifferent to his own earthly needs, and became unable to support his second wife and children. No one understood him, especially his wife, as he became more and more God-absorbed. His family began to live off the patronage of Tukaram's admirers.

The famous warrior king Shivaji, still a celebrated national hero, met Tukaram when he was in his late teens. Shivaji would visit Tukaram and was enchanted by listening to him read and sing his poems. Shivaji would watch Tukaram play his instrument and dance and Shivaji would not want to leave and attend to his kingly duties. It is said that Shivaji's mother would be forced to drag off her son, as nothing else could get him to depart except the humiliation of a king's mother berating him in front of his own subjects.

Many miracles are attributed to Tukaram, and he is often compared to St. Francis as animals and birds so loved him and he them. Birds often rode on his shoulders and sat on his instrument, which he kept slung around his neck when not playing it. With cymbals in hand and ecstatic tears on his face he would be seen in the streets dancing and singing his poems to God.

One day Tukaram playfully said to his close ones, "God is becoming jealous of the earth's love for me and He wonders if I would mind retiring from being so cute." Tukaram then informed his wife that God would be sending a taxi for him tomorrow and did she want to come. She declined saying, "Who would take care of our beautiful cows the way I do?"

The next day Tukaram invited some close ones to walk partway with him toward Bhandara. About halfway there he stopped, held their hands, and looking deep into their eyes with remarkable love, tenderly kissed each person, then walked off alone and was never seen again.

FIRST HE LOOKED CONFUSED

I could not lie anymore so I started to call my dog "God."
First he looked
confused,

then he started smiling, then he even
danced.

I kept at it: now he doesn't even
bite.

I am wondering if this
might work on
people?

A GOOD POEM

A good poem is like finding a hole
in the palace
wall—

never know what you
might
see.

I ASSAULTED THE HOLY ONE

I assaulted the Holy One
when he left the Tavern last night.
Boy, was He soused.

Lucky He wasn't
driving.

PROBABLY VERY THERAPEUTIC

God said
to me last night,

"Tuka, those love taunts won't work
in bringing my arms
near,

though I do find them amusing
and they are

probably
very

t
h
e
r
a
p
e
u
t
i
c
.
"

BECOMING WHOLE

The woman
whose speech and actions are the same—
her feet become worthy of
worship.

Keeping our word is the alchemy to become free
and whole.

Try and make amends for any broken hearts
or broken promises;

if you cannot do so in form
than prayer can heal a debt with the light you
can send,

and even a man can become
this precious
gold.

DID GOD REALLY SAY THE WORD *GOOFBALL*?

Did God
really call that famous leader a
goofball?

If
He did,
no need to worry about God anymore—
He is doing just
fine,

AND we are all a lot better off
than I earlier
suspected.

NO ONE WAS CRACKING THE KOANS

No one was cracking the koans
He had tattooed
everywhere.

So God changed His tactics—He developed a sweet tooth
and started chatting
about love.

He knew that really would not work and sure enough things got
worse—for a fine rebellious bunch we are.

This time people started stockpiling nukes,
and lawsuits plagued the land, and smog put a full nelson
on our lungs,

and T.V. hijacked brains, which caused millions to
vote Republican—
wow—

and all because we couldn't
bust a couple
koans.

THE EVERYTHING POEM

I am looking for a poem that says Everything
so I don't have to write
anymore.

HOW COULD A LOVER FALL?

What could have caused your grip to weaken
that allowed creation to be?

How could a lover fall to his death
from the arms of infinite
strength?

How active you are in the mind sustaining such a great wall
that the sun can cast a frightening shadow
the world believes.

No one has ever really known sadness. No real God
would ever allow pain.

How then can a heart feel it is broken and in need
if we are held in the arms of infinite
compassion and
strength?

That mirror you (God) stand before—
we need to gaze into it also.

That name you called Beloved
as I fell from your lips—
I suffer

because I did not quite
hear it;

so tell me again dear One
so clear:

I am

you.

THE SOURCE

God has never really spoken,
though a thought once crossed His mind.
It is the echo of divine
silence

we hear the birds sing, and that
is the source of all
we see and
touch.

GERONIMO

You might hear the beautiful shout of "Geronimo"
from a lover who has just dove from a
cliff and is heading full speed
into the Ocean—into the
Beloved.

And of course there will always be lots of gab
along the shore from those who are
drawn to God

but have yet to really get bare assed
and go in.

"Geronimo" may be the last word we hear
from that brave gal falling 625 MPH
from a cliff,

for once beneath the sea,
once within the
Water,

only fish open their mouths, still bargaining
for something.

The soul becomes quiet in ecstasy, so quiet.
Love speaks in absence of God,
not in the heights
of passion.

PREGNANT AGAIN

I think
the moon is pregnant again.

I hope she won't sue
me this
time.

LANDLOCKED IN FUR

I was meditating with my cat the other day
and all of a sudden she shouted,
"What happened?"

I knew exactly what she meant, but encouraged
her to say more—feeling that if she got it all out on the table
she would sleep better that night.

So I responded, "Tell me more, dear,"
and she soulfully meowed,

"Well, I was mingled with the sky. I was comets
whizzing here and there. I was suns in heat, hell—I was
galaxies. But now look—I am
landlocked in fur."

To this I said, "I know exactly what
you mean."

What to say about conversation
between

mystics?

DON'T BOTHER TO EVEN ASK

I
said to Love,

"I want to pull your pants down."

And She said,

"Fine! Don't bother to even ask."

Though now Tukaram is wondering

why there are so many sexually frustrated people

i
n

o
u
r

u
n
i
v
e
r
s
e

?
?
?

A PRIVATE STASH

I think God gave us the wrong
medicine.

Let's take a poll: How enlightened have you been feeling?

I bet He keeps a private stash
of something that
really

works.

CERTAINTY

Certainty undermines one's power, and turns happiness
into a long shot. Certainty confines.

Dears, there is nothing in your life that will not
change—especially all your ideas of God.

Look what the insanity of righteous knowledge can do:
crusade and maim thousands
in wanting to convert that which
is already gold
into gold.

Certainty can become an illness
that creates hate and
greed.

God once said to Tuka,

"Even I am ever changing—
I am ever beyond
Myself,

what I may have once put my seal upon,
may no longer be
the greatest
Truth."

THAT ANGEL TALKED LIKE A SAILOR

What part of heaven did she come from?
That angel talked like a sailor
and she was dressed
enchantingly
scant.

I can't even repeat the things she said,
or picture once more the shape of her breasts.

Though I know one thing:
My fear of dying has
vanished.

IT'S THE SHELL TRICK

It's the old shell trick with a twist:
I saw God put Himself in one
of your pockets.

You are bound
to find
Him.

I MIGHT ACT SERIOUS

If God would stop telling jokes,
I might act
serious.

BIRDS DON'T BRAG ABOUT FLYING

Birds
don't brag about flying
the way we
do.

They don't write books about it and then give
workshops,

they don't take on disciples and spoil
their own air
time.

Who could dance and achieve
liftoff with a bunch of
whackos tugging
on you?

MY LUCKY ROCK

I said to a squirrel, "What is that you are carrying?"
and he said,

"It is my lucky rock; isn't it pretty?"
I held it and said, "Indeed."

I said to God,

"What is this earth?"

And He said, "It is my lucky rock;
isn't it wondrous?"

Yes, indeed.

FEELING VERY SECURE

Some
planets rolled in
those openings on the side of my head.

I haven't heard anything for years.
Whenever I see a mouth moving in front of me

I just assume someone is saying
something brilliant

and then go on about my day
feeling very
secure.

LITTLE JABS THAT THEY ARE

"We should rumble," God said.

"I don't want to, I am too tired," I replied.

"Come on—give me your best shot,"
He persisted.

"Okay," I thought. So I hit Him with 8,000
poems,

little jabs that they are;

I didn't want
to hurt
the

Old

Guy.

A DELIRIOUS GANG

A
delirious gang
of club-bearing ants surrounded an elephant's house
and started shouting,

"You better watch out!"

I understand exactly what the elephant then thought:

Scholars, you are lucky
I am always
in a good
mood.

A FANCY EVENT

I
was invited
to a fancy event and when
I got there one of the guests said,

"Tukaram, your shirt is on backwards and so are
your pants,

and it looks like your hair never heard the word comb,
and your shoes don't
match."

I replied,

"Thanks, I noticed all that before leaving,
but why try to fool
anyone."

Works Consulted

Listed below are the primary English works that were remarkably helpful in crafting these poems. Some unpublished works, specifically that of Rumi and Hafiz, were invaluable in revealing some of their light. And several poems in this book I plucked from the field, my travels about the world, that led at times to serendipitous conversations about these great saints. I remember once on a flight to Jaipur, sitting next to a man who just a few nights ago sang Rumi poems till four in the morning, in a village that had been doing that for two centuries. I pinched a few lines from one of those songs; who published that book where he got the poem? Beats me. Thus the sources of some of this verse could be questioned, unless you come from the same school I hang out at: "where the heart is the chancellor because it knows, only that which can touch us is true."

RABIA

Halka, A. H. D. *Ralbi'a al-Adawiyya*. Argentina: Ediciones Dervish International, 1986.

Sakkakini, Widad El. *First Among Sufis, The Life and Thought of Rabia al-Adawiyya, the Woman Saint of Basra*. Translated by Dr. Nabil Safwat. London: The Octagon Press, 1982.

Smith, Margaret. *Rabia the Mystic and Her Fellow Saints in Islam*. San Francisco, CA: Rainbow Bridge, 1977. (First published in 1928 by Cambridge University Press.)

Stephens, William M. *Souls on Fire*. Nashville, TN: Oceanic Press, 1998.

Stewart-Wallace, Sir John, and Swami Ghanananda, editors. *Women Saints*. Hollywood, CA: Vendanta Press, 1955.

Upton, Charles. *Doorkeeper of the Heart: Versions of Rabi'a*. Putney, VT: Threshold Books, 1988.

ST. FRANCIS OF ASSISI

Allen, Paul M., and Joan deRis. *Francis of Assisi's Canticle of the Creatures*. New York: Continuum, 1996.

Butler, Salvator O.F.M., trans. *We Were with St. Francis*. Chicago: Franciscan Herald Press, 1976.

Chalippe, O.F.M., Father Candide, editor. *The Life and Legends of Saint Francis of Assisi*. New York: P. J. Kenedy & Sons, 1918. Revised and re-edited by Father Hilarion Duerk, O.F.M.

di Monte Santa Maria, Ugolino. *The Little Flowers of St. Francis of Assisi*. Translated by W. Heywood. New York: Vintage, 1998.

Klepec, O.S.F., Sister Elizabeth Marie, editor. *Daily Readings with St. Francis of Assisi*. Springfield, IL: Templegate Publishers, 1988.

Sabatier, Paul, editor. *The Life of St. Francis of Assisi*. Translated by Louise Seymour Houghton. New York: Charles Scribner's Sons, 1905.

Salvatorelli, Luigi. *The Life of St. Francis of Assisi*. Translated by Eric Sutton. New York: Knopf, 1928.

Talbot, John Michael, with Steve Rabey. *The Lessons of St. Francis*. New York: Dutton, 1998.

Van Balen Holt, Mary. *A Dwelling Place Within. 60 Reflections from the Writings of St. Francis*. Ann Arbor, MI: Charis, Servant Publications, 1999.

RUMI

Arberry, A. J., trans. *Discourses of Rumi*. York Beach, ME: Samuel Weiser Inc., 1977.

———. *Mystical Poems of Rumi*. Chicago and London: The University of Chicago Press, 1968.

Lewis, Franklin D. *Rumi: Past and Present, East and West*. Oxford, England: Oneworld Publications, 2000.

Nicholson, Reynold A., trans. *The Mathnawi of Jalalu'ddin' Rumi*. Reprint. London: Luzac & Co., 1977.

Nicholson, Reynold A., trans. *Rumi: Poet and Mystic*. London: George Allen and Unwin, 1950.

Stephens, William M. *Souls on Fire*. Nashville, TN: Oceanic Press, 1998.

MEISTER ECKHART

Ancelet-Hustache, Jeanne. *Meister Eckhart and the Rhineland Mystics*. Translated by Hilda Graef. London: Longmans, 1957.

Blakney, Raymond B., trans. *Meister Eckhart*. New York: Harper & Row, Publishers, Inc., 1941.

Evans, C. de B., trans. *The Works of Meister Eckhart: Doctor Ectaticus*. London: John M. Watkins, 1931.

Fleming, Ursula, editor. *Meister Eckhart, The Man from Whom God Nothing Hid*. Springfield, IL: Templegate Publishers, 1990.

Fox, Matthew, *One River Many Wells*. New York: Tarcher/Putnam, 2000.

Steiner, Rudolf. *Eleven European Mystics*. Translated by Karl E. Zimmer. New York: Rudolf Steiner Publications, 1960.

Walsh, M. O'C., comp. and trans. *Meister Eckhart, Sermons and Treatises*. Rockport, MA: Element, Inc., 1991.

ST. THOMAS AQUINAS

Chervin, Rhonda De Sola. *Quotable Saints*. Ann Arbor, MI: Servant Publications, 1992.

Chesterton, G. K. *Saint Thomas Aquinas*. New York: Doubleday, 1956.

Clark, Mary T., editor. *An Aquinas Reader*. New York: Fordham University Press, 1972.

Fox, Matthew. *One River Many Wells*. New York: Tarcher/Putnam, 2000.

Steiner, Rudolf. *Eleven European Mystics*. Translated by Karl E. Zimmer. New York: Rudolf Steiner Publications, 1960.

Vann, Joseph, O.F.M., editor. *Lives of Saints*. New York: John J. Crawley & Co., 1954.

HAFIZ

Arberry, Arthur J., trans. *Fifty Poems of Hafiz*. 1953. Reprint. Richmond, Surrey, UK: Curzon Press, 1993.

Bell, Gertrude Lowthian, trans. *Teachings of Hafiz*. 1897. Reprint. London: Octagon Press, 1979.

Clark, Lieut.-Col. H. Wilberforce, trans. *The Divan-i-Hafiz*. Two volumes. 1891. Reprint. York Beach, ME: Samuel Weiser, 1970.

Kennedy, Maud. *The Immortal Hafiz*. North Myrtle Beach, SC: Manifestation, 1987.

Nakosteen, Mehdi. *The Ghazaliyyat of Haafez of Shiraz*. Boulder, CO: Este Es Press, 1973.

Smith, Paul, trans. *Divan of Hafiz*. Two volumes. Melbourne: New Humanity Books, 1986.

Watkins, John M. *Selections from the Rubaiyat and Odes of Hafiz, Together with an Account of Sufi Mysticism*. 1920. Reprint. London: Stuart and Watkins, 1970.

ST. CATHERINE OF SIENA

Chervin, Rhonda De Sola. *Quotable Saints*. Ann Arbor, MI: Servant Publications, 1992.

Curtayne, Alice. *St. Catherine of Siena*. Rockford, IL: Tan Books, 1980.

Forbes, F. A. *Saint Catherine of Siena*. Rockford, IL: Tan Books, 1998.

Giordani, Igino. *Catherine of Siena*. Translated by Thomas J. Tobin. Milwaukee: The Bruce Publishing Co., 1959.

Stewart-Wallace, Sir John, and Swami Ghanananda, editors. *Women Saints*. Hollywood, CA: Vendanta Press, 1955.

Thorold, Algar, trans. *The Dialogue of Saint Catherine of Siena*. Rockford, IL: Tan Books, 1974.

Vann, Joseph, O.F.M., editor. *Lives of Saints*. New York: John J. Crawley & Co., 1954.

KABIR

Dass, Nirmal. *Songs of Kabir*. Delhi: Sri Satguru Publications, 1992.

Ezekiel, Isaac. *Kabir The Great Mystic*. Punjab, India: Radha Soami Satsang Beas, 1966.

Hess, Linda, and Shukdew Singh. *The Bijak of Kabir*. Delhi, India: Shri Jainendra Press, 1986.

Sawhney, Rajeev. *The Dialogues of Kabir*. Bangalore, India: UBS Publishers LTD, 1998.

Smith, Paul. *Kabir: Seven Hundred Sayings*. Melbourne: New Humanity Books, 1988.

Stephens, William M. *Souls on Fire*. Nashville, TN: Oceanic Press, 1998.

Tagore, Rabindranath. *Poems of Kabir*. Delhi, India: Raijv Beri, 1915.

Vaudeville, Charlotte. *A Weaver Named Kabir*. Calcutta, India: Oxford University Press, 1997.

MIRA

Alston, A. J. *The Devotional Poems of Mirabai*. Delhi, India: Shri Jainendra Press, 1980.

Levi, Louise. *Sweet on My Lips: The Love Poems of Mirabai*. Brooklyn, NY: Cool Grove Press, 1997.

Schelling, Andrew. *For Love of the Dark One: Songs of Mirabai*. Revised edition. Prescott, AZ: Hohm Press, 1998.

Stephens, William M. *Souls on Fire*. Nashville, TN: Oceanic Press, 1998.

Stewart-Wallace, Sir John, and Swami Ghanananda, editors. *Women Saints*. Hollywood, CA: Vendanta Press, 1955.

ST. TERESA OF AVILA

Hamilton, Elizabeth. *The Life of Saint Teresa of Avila*. Westminster, MD: Christian Classics, 1985.

Harvey, Andrew. *Teachings of the Christian Mystics*. Boston, MA: Shambhala, 1998.

Kavanaugh, O.C.D., Kieran, and Otilio Rodriguez, O.C.D., trans. *The Collected Works of St. Teresa of Avila, Volume One: The Book of Her Life, Spiritual Testimonies and Soliloquies*. Washington, D.C.: ICS Publications, Institute of Carmelite Studies, 1976. Second Edition, 1987.

——. *The Collected Works of St. Teresa of Avila, Volume Two: The Way of Perfection, Meditations on the "Song of Songs," The Interior Castle*. Washington, D.C.: ICS Publications, Institute of Carmelite Studies, 1976. Second Edition, 1980.

——. *The Collected Works of St. Teresa of Avila, Volume Three: The Book of Her Foundations, Minor Works*. Washington, D.C.: ICS Publications, Institute of Carmelite Studies, 1985.

Peers, E. Allison, trans. *The Way of Perfection, Teresa of Avila*. New York: Doubleday, 1964.

———. *The Life of Teresa of Jesus*. New York: Doubleday, 1960.

Pond, Kathleen, trans. *The Spirit of the Spanish Mystics*. New York: P. J. Kenedy & Sons, 1958.

Stephens, William M. *Souls on Fire*. Nashville, TN: Oceanic Press, 1998.

ST. JOHN OF THE CROSS

Barnstone, Willis, trans. *The Poems of St. John of the Cross*. New York: New Directions, 1968.

Kavanaugh, O.C.D., Kieran, and Otilio Rodriguez, O.C.D., trans. *The Collected Works of St. John of the Cross*. Washington, D.C.: ICS Publications, Institute of Carmelite Studies, 1973.

Nicolas, Antonio T. de, trans. *St. John of the Cross: Alchemist of the Soul*. York Beach, ME, 1996.

Nims, John Frederick, trans. *The Poems of St. John of the Cross: New English Versions*. New York: Grove Press, 1959.

Peers, E. Allison, trans. *Dark Night of the Soul by St. John of the Cross*. New York: Doubleday, 1959.

Ruth, Sister Elizabeth, O.D.C., editor. *Daily Readings with St. John of the Cross*. Springfield, IL: Templegate Publishers, 1986.

TUKARAM

Chitre, Dilip. *Tukaram: Says Tuka*. New Delhi, India: Penguin Books, 1991.

Fraser, J. Nelson, and K. B. Marathe. *The Poems of Tukaram*. New Delhi, India: Shri Jainendra Press, 1909.

Macnicol, Nicol. *Psalms of Maratha Saints: One Hundred and Eight Hymns translated from the Marathi*. Calcutta, India: Oxford University Press, 1919.

Index of Titles

Index of First Lines

Something inside said I was a
   mineral, and I was so glad to
   just be, 84
Sometimes we think what we are
   saying about God, 148
Stuck with another day, 260
Such love does, 48

Tenderly, I now touch all things,
   325
The Christ said to us, 149
The earth and sky will open
   their purse for you, 285
The earth looked at Him and
   began to dance, 267
The experience of something out
   of nothing—, 133
The force that created the
   unimaginable splendors, 192
The grass beneath a tree is con-
   tent, 82
The limbs of a tree reached
   down and lifted me, 141
The moment's depth is greater
   than that of, 8
The moon and I, 219
The moon was once a moth who
   ran to her lover, 22
The moon was perched like a
   golden hawk, 252
The rejected lover trembles,
   258
The result of prayer is life, 54
The sadness I have caused any
   face, 81
The sky gave me its heart, 9
The sun hears the fields talking
   about effort, 195
The weight of arrogance is such,
   320

The woman whose speech and
   actions are the same, 337
The wonder of water moving
   over that rock in the stream,
   77
The words Guru, Swami, Super
   Swami, Master, Teacher, Mur-
   shid, 217
There are beautiful wild forces
   within us, 47
There are seasons in the mind,
   218
There are so many positions of
   love, 156
There is a beautiful creature liv-
   ing, 174
There is a dog I sometimes take
   for a walk, 20
There is a sword in a museum
   not far from me, 239
There is dew, 225
These just aren't words you are
   reading, 63
They are always kissing, 100
They are like shy, young school
   kids, 287
They can be a great help, 110
They can be like a sun, words,
   324
They kiss sometimes when no
   one is looking, 187
Three years went by, 261
Troubled?, 168
Truth never frightens, 202

Vulnerable we are, like an infant,
   185

We bless the earth with each
   step we take, 51

ALSO AVAILABLE

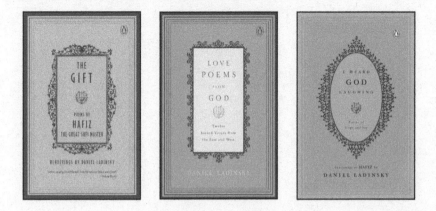

DARLING, I LOVE YOU

Poems from the Hearts of Our Glorious Mutts and All Our Animal Friends

THE GIFT

Poems by Hafiz, the Great Sufi Master
Renderings of Hafiz by Daniel Ladinsky

I HEARD GOD LAUGHING

Poems of Hope and Joy
Renderings of Hafiz by Daniel Ladinsky

LOVE POEMS FROM GOD

Twelve Sacred Voices from the East and West
Renderings by Daniel Ladinsky

THE PURITY OF DESIRE

100 Poems of Rumi
Renderings of Rumi by Daniel Ladinsky with Nancy Owen Barton

THE SUBJECT TONIGHT IS LOVE

60 Wild and Sweet Poems of Hafiz
Renderings of Hafiz by Daniel Ladinsky

A YEAR WITH HAFIZ

Daily Contemplations
Renderings of Hafiz by Daniel Ladinsky

 PENGUIN BOOKS

Ready to find your next great read? Let us help. Visit prh.com/nextread

9 780142 196120

CPSIA information can be obtained
at www.ICGtesting.com
Printed in the USA
LVHW040146080221
678685LV00015B/992